W9-BMZ-338

THE CHRISTMAS COOKBOOK

OVER 150 FESTIVE RECIPES

THE
CHRISTMAS
COOKBOOK

OVER 150 FESTIVE RECIPES

**BEDFORD
EDITIONS**

Recipes and photographs on the following pages are credited as follows:
Copyright of Merehurst Press:
64l, 65l, 66l, 66r, 67l, 67r, 68l, 68r, 69l, 69r, 70l, 70r, 71, 72l, 72r, 73l, 73r.
Copyright of Beverley Sutherland Smith, by arrangement with Merehurst Press:
77l, 77r, 82l, 82r, 83l, 83r, 84l, 84r, 85l, 85r, 86l, 86r, 87l, 87r.
Copyright of Annette Grimsdale, by arrangement with Merehurst Press:
20l, 20r, 22l, 22r, 23, 24l, 24r, 25l, 25r, 35l, 35r, 62l, 62r, 78l, 78r, 79l, 79r, 80l, 80r,
81l, 81r, 90l, 90r, 91l, 91r, 92l, 92r, 93l, 93r, 94l, 94r, 95l, 95r.

Compiled by: Brown Packaging

Contributing authors: Pat Alburey, Annette Grimsdale,
Janice Murfitt, Beverley Sutherland Smith.

Photographers: Paul Grater, Ray Joyce, Jon Stewart, Philip Wymant.

ISBN: 0-86101-734-X

Printed in Italy

CONTENTS

Introduction
page 6

Party Food & Drink
pages 7-28

Lunches & Dinners
pages 29-40

Puddings, Desserts, & Cakes
pages 41-62

Cookies, Candies, & Gifts
pages 63-95

Index
page 96

INTRODUCTION

Christmas is the most wonderful time of year when family and friends meet to celebrate this happy occasion. Everything seems to buzz with excitement as the festivities fill the air — and the time should be one of happiness and giving.

However, so often as Christmas approaches, panic surrounds us and thoughts of how to plan the food; what to cook; how much to make, and so on ... fill our minds. *The Christmas Cookbook* is designed to help answer these questions and includes all manner of recipes relating to the festive season from traditional Christmas fare, such as the dinner and accompaniments, to cakes, puddings, and mince pies, plus delicious alternatives, and much, much more.

You will find simple recipes to make and freeze ahead of time; delicious desserts and puddings to impress your family and guests and a range of eye-catching canapés to serve with drinks or to make, in quantity, for a party. There's also a wonderful selection of cakes and cookies which offers a range of lovely ideas, including some novelty ones for children.

And, last but not least, there's a delightful selection of decorations and gifts to make ahead of time — which are fun to do for both adults and children and are sure to bring you compliments!

The Christmas Cookbook has over 150 delicious recipes — each and every one illustrated with colorful and informative step-by-step photographs to guide you to success every time. Each recipe section has been planned to make Christmas much easier, simply by containing a selection of ideas to suit all occasions and help make Christmas a deliciously trouble-free, happy occasion.

PARTY FOOD & DRINK

Bacon Aigrettes

4 slices bacon
1 tablespoon chopped fresh parsley
1/2 teaspoon ground black pepper
1/2 teaspoon Dijon-style mustard
Oil for frying

Choux Pastry:
2/3 cup water
1/4 cup butter
1/2 cup all-purpose flour
2 eggs

Dip:
2/3 cup plain yogurt
1 tablespoon chopped chives
1 tablespoon mango chutney

Cook bacon until crisp and chop finely. In a bowl, mix together bacon, parsley, pepper and mustard.

To prepare pastry, in a saucepan, heat water and butter until melted. Bring to a boil, remove pan from heat and immediately add all flour, beating vigorously to form a paste. Return to heat for a few seconds, stirring until paste forms a ball. Add eggs 1 at a time, beating until paste is very smooth and glossy. Stir in bacon mixture until well blended.

Half-fill a deep saucepan with oil. Heat to 360F (180C), or test by dropping small pieces of paste into oil. If it sizzles on contact, oil is hot enough. Drop teaspoonfuls of mixture into hot oil. Fry 3 to 4 minutes, turning once, or until puffed and golden brown. Drain on paper towels. Arrange on a serving dish. To prepare dip, mix yogurt, chives and chutney in a bowl. Serve with Bacon Aigrettes. Makes 35 to 40 pieces.

Asparagus in Chicory Leaves

8 oz. asparagus spears, trimmed
3 heads chicory
1 (8-oz.) pkg. cream cheese
3 slices proscuitto or parma ham
Tangerine wedges and dill sprigs to garnish

Marinade:
1 tangerine
1/2 clove garlic, crushed
1/4 teaspoon salt
1/4 teaspoon ground black pepper
1/2 teaspoon Dijon-style mustard
2 teaspoons honey
1 tablespoon plus 1 teaspoon olive oil
2 teaspoons chopped fresh tarragon

Half-fill a shallow skillet with water; bring to a boil. Add asparagus and cook 3 to 4 minutes or until spears are tender. Drain and cool in a shallow dish.

To prepare marinade, using a zester, cut peel of tangerine into fine strips; squeeze juice into a bowl. Add garlic, salt, pepper, mustard, honey, oil and tarragon and beat with a wooden spoon until thoroughly blended. Pour over asparagus, cover and chill for at least 1 hour.

Separate chicory leaves and cut in 1-inch lengths. Spread a little cream cheese onto each leaf. Cut asparagus spears in 1-inch lengths; place a piece of asparagus onto each chicory leaf. Cut proscuitto or ham in thin strips and wrap a piece around each chicory leaf. Garnish with tangerine wedges and dill sprigs. Makes 48 pieces.

Curried Vegetable Envelopes

2 oz. puff pastry, thawed
1 egg, beaten
1 teaspoon cumin seeds
Lime twists and herb sprigs to garnish

Filling:
1 tablespoon butter
1 leek, finely chopped
1 clove garlic, crushed
1 teaspoon ground cumin
1 teaspoon garam marsala
2 teaspoons mango chutney
1/2 teaspoon finely grated lime peel
2 teaspoons lime juice
1/2 cup cooked diced potato

Preheat oven to 425F (220C). To prepare filling, melt butter in small saucepan. Add leek and garlic.

Cook quickly, stirring, 1 minute. Add cumin, garam marsala, chutney and lime peel and juice. Stir well. Cook gently 1 to 2 minutes. Add potatoes, mix well and cool. Roll out puff pastry very thinly to a 12" x 8" rectangle. Cut in 2-inch squares. Brush edge with beaten egg and place a little filling in center of each square.

Draw all corners to center and seal joins like a tiny envelope. Arrange on a baking sheet. Brush envelopes with egg to glaze and sprinkle with cumin seeds. Bake in oven 5 to 8 minutes or until well risen and golden brown. Garnish with lime twists and herb sprigs. Makes 24 pieces.

Oysters with Eggplant

1 cup diced eggplant
Salt
6 large slices white bread
1/4 cup butter
2 tablespoons snipped chives
2 teaspoons chopped fresh oregano
4 button mushrooms, finely chopped
1/2 teaspoon ground black pepper
2 teaspoons fromage frais
12 fresh oysters in shells
3/4 cup soft bread crumbs
Oregano sprigs to garnish

Place eggplant in a bowl. Sprinkle with salt. Cover and let stand 30 minutes.

Preheat oven to 425F (220C). Cut crusts off bread. Roll slices flat with a rolling pan. Cut in 24 (2-inch) rounds using a daisy cutter. Spread both sides with some butter and press into muffin pans. Bake in oven 5 minutes or until lightly browned.

Drain and rinse eggplant. Dry on paper towels. Melt remaining butter in a saucepan. Add eggplant, chives, chopped oregano, mushrooms, pepper and some salt. Fry quickly, stirring occasionally, until eggplant is tender. Stir in fromage frais. Scrub oyster shells. Open and remove oysters. Cut each in half and place a half into each bread cup. Top with eggplant mixture and sprinkle with bread crumbs. Return to oven 10 minutes or until bread crumbs are lightly browned. Garnish with oregano sprigs. Makes 24 pieces.

Oatie Brie Cubes

1-1/2 cups soft bread crumbs
1/4 cup regular oatmeal
1/2 teaspoon salt
1/2 teaspoon ground black pepper
1/2 teaspoon dry mustard
2 eggs
8 oz. firm Brie or Camembert cheese
Oil for frying
Bay leaves, cranberries and lime wedges to
    garnish

Dip:
3/4 cup cranberries
Grated peel and juice 1 lime
1 tablespoon superfine sugar

In a bowl, mix bread crumbs, oatmeal, salt, pepper and mustard. Beat eggs in a small bowl.

Cut cheese in bite-sized cubes. Place 1 cube at time into beaten eggs, then coat evenly in oatmeal mixture. Repeat to coat all cheese cubes. Repeat to coat cheese cubes a second time in eggs and oatmeal mixture. Chill until needed.

To prepare dip, place cranberries and lime peel and juice in a saucepan. Bring to a boil, cover and cook 1 to 2 minutes until cranberries are tender. In a food processor fitted with a metal blade, process cranberry mixture and sugar until smooth. Pour into a small serving dish. Half-fill a saucepan with oil. Heat to 350F (175C) or when a cheese cube sizzles immediately. Fry about 6 cheese cubes at a time until pale golden. Drain on paper towels. Garnish with bay leaves, cranberries and lime wedges. Serve with dip. Makes 20 pieces.

Crab & Fennel Puffs

1 recipe Choux Pastry, page 8
1 egg yolk, beaten
2 teaspoons sesame seeds
Fennel sprigs and radish slices to garnish
Cayenne pepper

Filling:
1 tablespoon butter
3 tablespoons finely chopped green onions
3 tablespoons finely chopped fennel
1/3 cup white crab meat
1/4 cup dark crab meat
1/2 teaspoon finely grated lemon peel
1/4 teaspoon ground black pepper
1 tablespoon sour cream
Cayenne pepper

Preheat oven to 425F (220C). Grease 2 baking sheets.

Place pastry in a piping bag fitted with a 1/2-inch plain nozzle. Pipe about 40 small rounds of pastry, spacing apart, onto greased baking sheets. Brush with egg yolk and sprinkle with sesame seeds. Bake in oven 15 to 20 minutes or until crisp and golden brown. Cool on a wire rack. To prepare filling, melt butter in a small saucepan. Add green onion and fennel. Cook 1 to 2 minutes or until tender. Remove pan from heat. Stir in light and dark crab meat, lemon peel, pepper and sour cream until well blended.

Cut each pastry ball across top. Fill each with crab filling and dust with cayenne pepper. Arrange on a serving plate. Garnish with fennel sprigs and radish slices. Makes 40 pieces.

Cheese Straws

Cheese Pastry:
2 cups all-purpose flour
1/2 teaspoon salt
1/2 teaspoon cayenne pepper
1/2 teaspoon dry mustard
1/2 cup butter
1 cup shredded Cheddar cheese (4 oz.)
1 egg, beaten

Flavorings:
1 tablespoon plus 1 teaspoon finely chopped red and yellow bell peppers
1 clove garlic, crushed
1 tablespoon plus 1 teaspoon chopped fresh basil
1 tablespoon plus 1 teaspoon chopped fresh parsley
Red and yellow bell pepper twists and bay leaves to garnish

Preheat oven to 400F (205C). Grease several baking sheets. In a bowl, sift flour, salt, cayenne and mustard. Cut butter into pieces. Cut butter into flour mixture finely to resemble bread crumbs. Using a fork, stir in cheese and egg until mixture clings together. Knead to a smooth dough.

Cut pastry in 4 pieces. Flavor 1 piece with peppers, 1 with garlic, 1 with basil and remaining piece with parsley, kneading each piece lightly. Roll out 1 piece at a time to a 4-inch-wide strip that is 1/4-inch thick.

Using a knife, cut in 1/4-inch strips. Arrange in a straight line on greased baking sheets. Knead each of flavored trimmings together, re-roll and cut out rings using a 2-inch and 1-1/2-inch plain cutter. Place on baking sheets. Bake in oven 5 to 8 minutes or until golden. Cool on wire racks. Serve straws in bundles threaded through pastry rings. Garnish with bell pepper twists and bay leaves. Makes 100 pieces.

Crispy Pesto Shrimp

12 cooked peeled jumbo shrimp
6 large slices white bread
1/4 cup butter
1 clove garlic
1 tablespoon plus 1 teaspoon pesto sauce
1 teaspoon finely grated lemon peel
1/4 teaspoon salt
1/4 teaspoon ground black pepper
Lemon triangles and lemon balm leaves to garnish

Cut each shrimp in half across width. Cut crusts off bread. Using a rolling pin, roll each slice flat.

In a small bowl, beat butter until soft and smooth. Stir in garlic, pesto sauce, lemon peel, salt and pepper. Beat until smooth and well blended. Spread both sides of each slice of bread with butter mixture and cut each slice in 4 triangles.

Place a shrimp in center of each bread triangle. Fold 2 points to center and secure with a wooden pick. Arrange on a grid in a grill pan and broil under a moderately hot grill until bread is lightly browned. Garnish with lemon triangles and lemon balm leaves and serve hot. Makes 24 pieces.

Festive Dip Selection

Curry Whirls

1 small eggplant
2 cloves garlic
1/2 cup sour cream
Salt
Ground black pepper
1 tablespoon chopped fresh rosemary
1 (8-oz.) pkg. cream cheese
2 tablespoons fromage frais
1/4 cup chopped fresh mixed herbs such as
    parsley, basil, thyme, oregano and chervil
2/3 cup red lentils
1-3/4 cups water
2/3 cup plain yogurt
Mixed vegetable sticks (zucchini, bell peppers,
    celery, cucumbers, carrots) baby sweet corn,
    cherry tomatoes and radishes

1-1/4 cups all-purpose flour
1 teaspoon curry powder
1/2 teaspoon salt
1/2 teaspoon pepper
1/2 teaspoon dry mustard
1/2 cup butter
2 tablespoons Parmesan cheese
1 egg, beaten
1 teaspoon coriander seeds
Tomato wedges and parsley to garnish

Preheat oven to 425F (220C) or use a hot grill. Bake or grill eggplant until skin has charred and flesh is tender, turning once. Cut eggplant in half, scoop out flesh, cool. Using a food processor fitted with a metal blade, process eggplant, 1 clove of garlic, sour cream, salt and pepper to taste and rosemary until mixture is smooth and creamy. Spoon into a serving bowl.

Place cream cheese, fromage frais, herbs and salt and pepper to taste in a bowl. Beat until soft and well blended. Spoon into a serving dish.

In a saucepan, bring lentils and water to a boil, then simmer gently until all water has been absorbed. Cool. In food processor, process lentils, remaining garlic, salt, pepper and yogurt until creamy and smooth. Spoon into a serving dish. Serve dips with mixed vegetables. Each dip makes 6 to 8 servings.

Preheat oven to 425F(220C). Lightly grease several baking sheets. In a bowl, sift flour, curry powder, salt, pepper and mustard. Cut butter in pieces. Cut butter into flour mixture finely to resemble bread crumbs. Using a fork, stir in Parmesan cheese and egg until mixture clings together. Mix to a soft dough.

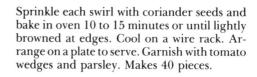

Place mixture in a pastry bag fitted with a star nozzle. Pipe about 40 swirls of mixture onto lightly greased baking sheets, spacing apart.

Sprinkle each swirl with coriander seeds and bake in oven 10 to 15 minutes or until lightly browned at edges. Cool on a wire rack. Arrange on a plate to serve. Garnish with tomato wedges and parsley. Makes 40 pieces.

Stuffed Leaves

10 small spinach leaves
10 small lettuce leaves
10 small radicchio leaves

Filling:
5 slices bacon
1 tablespoon plus 1 teaspoon chopped pickled
    vegetables
2 oz. Neufchâtel cheese
1/4 cup cooked white long-grain rice
1 teaspoon Dijon-style mustard
1/2 teaspoon salt
1/2 teaspoon ground black pepper
1 small red bell pepper, seeded
1 small yellow bell pepper, seeded

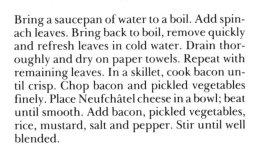

Bring a saucepan of water to a boil. Add spinach leaves. Bring back to boil, remove quickly and refresh leaves in cold water. Drain thoroughly and dry on paper towels. Repeat with remaining leaves. In a skillet, cook bacon until crisp. Chop bacon and pickled vegetables finely. Place Neufchâtel cheese in a bowl; beat until smooth. Add bacon, pickled vegetables, rice, mustard, salt and pepper. Stir until well blended.

Spread leaves out flat on a board. Place 1 teaspoonful of mixture on each leaf. Roll up and secure each with a wooden pick. Cut bell peppers in thin rings; cut rings in 4 pieces. Arrange stuffed leaves on a serving plate. Garnish with bell peppers. Makes 30 pieces.

Feta Cheese Kebabs

7 oz. feta cheese
1/4 red bell pepper
1/4 yellow bell pepper
1 zucchini
1/4 eggplant
Thyme sprigs and pink peppercorns

Marinade:
2 tablespoons olive oil
1 tablespoon raspberry vinegar
1 teaspoon honey
1/2 teaspoon Dijon-style mustard
2 teaspoons chopped fresh thyme
1/4 teaspoon salt
1/2 teaspoon ground black pepper

To prepare marinade, combine olive oil, vinegar, peppercorns, honey, mustard, thyme, salt and pepper in a large bowl with a wooden spoon until thoroughly blended. Cut feta cheese, bell peppers, zucchini and eggplant in bite-sized pieces. Add to marinade; stir well to coat evenly. Cover with plastic wrap and refrigerate at least 1 hour.

Thread 1 piece of each ingredient onto wooden picks. Just before serving, broil under a hot grill 2 to 3 minutes or until vegetables are just tender. Garnish with thyme sprigs and peppercorns. Makes 24 kebabs.

Chicken Liver Pouches

2 leaves phyllo or streudel pastry, thawed
1/4 cup butter, melted
1 teaspoon poppy seeds
Oregano sprigs and tomato wedges to garnish

Filling:
1 tablespoon butter
1 clove garlic, crushed
4 oz. chicken livers
1 tablespoon chopped fresh oregano
1/4 teaspoon salt
1/4 teaspoon ground black pepper
2 teaspoons all-purpose flour
2 teaspoons Marsala wine
2 tablespoons half and half

Preheat oven to 400F (205C). Line 2 baking sheets with parchment paper. To prepare filling, melt butter in a small saucepan. Add chicken livers and garlic and fry quickly 30 seconds. Stir in oregano, salt, pepper and flour until well blended. Add wine and half and half. Bring to a boil, stirring constantly. Remove from heat and cool.

Brush pastry sheets with melted butter; place one on top of the other. Using a sharp knife, cut pastry in 2-1/2-inch squares. Spoon a little filling onto each square. Draw up corners of pastry and press firmly together. Press down slightly to flatten. Brush each pouch with remaining butter and sprinkle with poppy seeds. Place pouches on prepared baking sheet. Bake in oven 5 minutes or until golden brown. Arrange on a warmed serving dish. Garnish with oregano sprigs and tomato wedges. Makes 24 pieces.

Cocktail Pinwheels

2-1/4 cups all-purpose flour
1/2 teaspoon salt
1/2 teaspoon cayenne pepper
1 teaspoon dry mustard
3/4 cup butter
1 cup shredded Cheddar cheese (4 oz.)
1 egg, beaten
Parsley sprigs to garnish

Flavorings:
1 teaspoon sesame seeds
1 teaspoon poppy seeds
1 teaspoon curry paste
2 teaspoons tomato paste

In a bowl, sift flour, salt, cayenne and mustard. Cut butter in pieces. Cut butter into flour mixture finely to resemble bread crumbs. Using a fork, stir in cheese and egg until mixture clings together. Knead in a smooth dough.

Cut pastry in 4 pieces. Knead sesame seeds into 1 piece and poppy seeds into another. Form both in 6-inch rolls. Wrap separately in plastic wrap. Roll remaining 2 pieces of pastry in 8" x 6" rectangles. Spread 1 piece with curry paste and other with tomato paste. Roll up each from long edge in 2 firm rolls. Wrap in plastic wrap. Chill until firm or freeze until needed.

Preheat oven to 400F (205C). Line several baking sheets with parchment paper. Cut each roll in thin slices and arrange a little apart on prepared baking sheets. Bake for 6 to 8 minutes or until golden. Cool, then transfer to wire racks. Garnish with parsley sprigs. Makes 96 pieces.

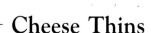

Lamb & Walnut Bites

8 oz. lamb fillet, cut up
1 cup soft bread crumbs
1 shallot
2 teaspoons fresh rosemary
1 teaspoon salt
1/2 teaspoon ground black pepper
1 egg
5 pickled walnuts
All-purpose flour
Rosemary sprigs to garnish

Sauce:
1 onion, finely chopped
1 clove garlic, crushed
3 large tomatoes, peeled, seeded, chopped
1 tablespoon chopped fresh basil
Oil for frying

In a food processor fitted with a metal blade, process lamb until finely chopped. Add bread crumbs, shallot, rosemary, salt, pepper and egg. Process until smooth. Cut pickled walnuts in small pieces. Using a little flour, press 1 teaspoonful of meat mixture in a flat round. Place a piece of walnut in center and form in a smooth ball. Repeat to make about 35 to 40 balls.

To prepare sauce, combine onion, garlic and tomatoes in a small saucepan. Bring to a boil and cook rapidly, stirring occasionally, until mixture is pulpy and thick. Stir in basil and pour into a serving dish. Half-fill a small pan with oil. Heat to 350F (175C) or to when a meat ball is placed in oil, it sizzles immediately. Fry meat balls in several batches 2 to 3 minutes or until lightly browned. Drain on paper towels. Serve with sauce. Garnish with rosemary sprigs. Makes 35 to 40 pieces.

Cheese Thins

1 cup all-purpose flour
1/2 teaspoon salt
1/2 teaspoon pepper
1/2 teaspoon dry mustard
1/2 cup butter
1 cup shredded Cheddar cheese (4 oz.)
1 tablespoon plus 1 teaspoon regular oats
1 teaspoon cayenne pepper
1 egg white
Fennel sprigs to garnish

Preheat oven to 425F (220C). Lightly grease 2 baking sheets. Sift flour, salt, pepper and mustard into a bowl. Cut butter into pieces. Cut butter into flour mixture finely until mixture begins to cling together.

Using a fork, stir in cheese and mix to a soft dough. Knead on a lightly floured surface and roll out very thinly. Using a 1-inch oval cutter, cut out 80 oval shapes. Arrange on greased baking sheets, spacing apart.

In a small bowl, mix oatmeal and cayenne. Brush each oval with egg white and sprinkle with oatmeal mixture. Bake in oven to 5 to 6 minutes or until pale in color. Cool on baking sheets a few minutes, then remove carefully with a palette knife. Arrange on a plate to serve. Garnish with fennel sprigs. Makes 80 pieces.

Herbed Crepe Pinwheels

1/2 cup all-purpose flour
1/4 teaspoon salt
1/4 teaspoon ground black pepper
1 egg
1/4 cup milk
1 tablespoon fresh chopped basil
Oil
Cherry tomato wedges and herb sprigs to
  garnish

Filling:
8 large spinach leaves
1/2 (8-oz.) pkg. cream cheese with herbs and
  garlic, softened
8 thin slices proscuitto or Parma ham

To prepare batter, sift flour, salt and pepper
into a bowl. Mix in egg and 1/2 of milk with a
wooden spoon; beat until smooth. Stir in
remaining milk and basil. Beat until well
blended.

Heat a little oil in a small skillet. Add 1 spoonful of batter; swirl pan to coat thinly. Cook
until crepe is pale golden on both sides, turning only once. Place on paper towels. Repeat
to make 8 crepes.

In a saucepan, cook spinach leaves 1 minute
in boiling salted water. Drain and cool. Cover
1 crepe with a spinach leaf, spread with some
cream cheese and cover with a slice of proscuitto or Parma ham. Roll up firmly and
wrap in plastic wrap. Repeat to make 8 crepe
rolls. Just before serving, cut each roll in 1/2-
inch slices. Arrange on a serving plate. Garnish with cherry tomato wedges and herb
sprigs. Makes 48 pinwheels.

Party Quiches

1/2 cup all-purpose flour
1/4 teaspoon salt
2 teaspoons butter
2 to 3 teaspoons cold water
Red bell pepper rings and fennel sprigs to
  garnish

Filling:
1 egg
2 tablespoons half and half
1/4 teaspoon salt
1/4 teaspoon pepper
1/4 teaspoon dry mustard
2 teaspoons finely chopped bell peppers,
2 teaspoons chopped button mushrooms
2 teaspoons chopped crispy bacon
2 teaspoons chopped fresh herbs

Sift flour and salt into a bowl. Cut butter in
pieces. Cut butter into flour mixture finely
until mixture resembles bread crumbs. Using
a fork, stir in water until mixture begins to
bind together. Knead to a firm dough.

Roll out pastry thinly on a lightly floured surface. Line 24 tiny pastry boat molds or tiny
round tart pans with pastry. Prick pastry and
chill 1 hour. Preheat oven to 425F (220C).
Bake pastry molds in oven 5 minutes, then
remove from oven.

To prepare filling, place egg, half and half,
salt, pepper and mustard into a bowl. Whisk
until well blended. Half-fill each pastry with
egg mixture, then fill with chopped bell peppers, mushrooms, bacon and herbs. Return to
oven 5 to 6 minutes or until filling has set.
Cool slightly, then slip pastry out of molds.
Serve warm or cold. Garnish with bell pepper
rings and fennel sprigs. Makes 24 pieces.

Mussels with Tomato Sauce

Creamy Filled Quail Eggs

12 fresh mussels
2 tablespoons butter
2 tomatoes, peeled, seeded, chopped
2 tablespoons chopped chives
2 tablespoons chopped fresh basil
1 clove garlic, crushed
1 tablespoon tomato paste
1/4 teaspoon salt
1/4 teaspoon ground black pepper
1/2 teaspoon sugar
6 slices brown bread
2 tablespoons vegetable oil
3 pitted prunes, cut in pieces, and basil leaves
   to garnish

12 quail eggs
4 large slices whole-wheat toast
1 tablespoon butter
2 teaspoons red lumpfish caviar and dill sprigs
   to garnish

Filling:
1/3 cup cooked garbanzo beans
2 tablespoons whipping cream
1/2 teaspoon salt
1/2 teaspoon ground black pepper
1 teaspoon Dijon-style mustard

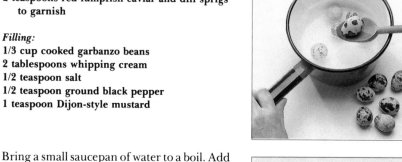

Scrub mussels and remove beards. Place in a saucepan, cover and heat gently until shells have opened. Cool and discard any mussels that do not open. To prepare sauce, melt butter in a saucepan. Stir in tomatoes, chives, basil, garlic, tomato paste, salt, pepper and sugar. Bring to a boil, stirring occasionally. Cook gently 2 minutes or until thick.

Bring a small saucepan of water to a boil. Add quail eggs and cook 3 minutes. Drain and cover with cold water. Peel and cut in halves. Scoop out yolks.

To prepare filling, in a food processor fitted with a metal blade, process garbanzo beans until smooth. Add egg yolks, whipping cream, salt, pepper and mustard and process until smooth and creamy. Place filling in a pastry bag fitted with a small star nozzle. Pipe swirls of mixture into egg whites.

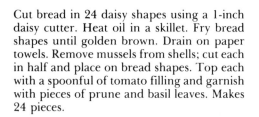

Cut bread in 24 daisy shapes using a 1-inch daisy cutter. Heat oil in a skillet. Fry bread shapes until golden brown. Drain on paper towels. Remove mussels from shells; cut each in half and place on bread shapes. Top each with a spoonful of tomato filling and garnish with pieces of prune and basil leaves. Makes 24 pieces.

Cut toast in tiny ovals or rounds using a 1-inch cutter. Spread thinly with butter and sit a filled egg on each. Garnish with a little lumpfish caviar and dill sprigs. Makes 24 pieces.

Crispy Bacon Pinwheels

3/4 cup shredded Cheddar cheese (3 oz.)
1/4 teaspoon salt
1/4 teaspoon pepper
1/2 teaspoon Dijon-style mustard
2 tablespoons plain yogurt
6 large slices white bread
3 tablespoons butter
6 slices bacon
Celery leaves and radish slices to garnish

In a bowl, mix cheese, salt, pepper, mustard and yogurt. Cut crusts off bread; roll slices flat with a rolling pin. Spread each slice with butter and invert. Spread unbuttered sides evenly with cheese mixture and roll each up in a firm roll.

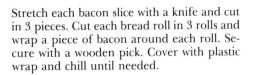

Stretch each bacon slice with a knife and cut in 3 pieces. Cut each bread roll in 3 rolls and wrap a piece of bacon around each roll. Secure with a wooden pick. Cover with plastic wrap and chill until needed.

Just before serving, broil bacon rolls under a hot grill until bacon is crisp and golden brown. Cool slightly, remove wooden picks and cut each roll in 3 slices. Garnish with celery and radish slices. Makes 54 pinwheels.

—Marinated Mushrooms with Grapefruit–

1 large pink grapefruit
1/3 cup ginger wine
2 teaspoons mint jelly
1/2 teaspoon salt
1/2 teaspoon ground black pepper
1 teaspoon Dijon-style mustard
48 button mushrooms
Mint leaves to garnish

Using a sharp knife, cut away grapefruit peel including white pith from flesh, allowing juice to fall into a small saucepan. Cut out segments in between membranes and place on a plate. Squeeze remaining juice from membranes into saucepan.

Stir in ginger wine, mint jelly, salt, pepper and mustard. Bring to a boil. Stir in mushrooms. Pour into a bowl and refrigerate until cold.

Cut grapefruit segments in bite-sized pieces. Reserve several grapefruit pieces for garnish. Thread mushrooms and grapefruit onto 24 wooden picks. Garnish with mint leaves and reserved grapefruit pieces. Makes 24 pieces.

Avocado Salmon Rolls

3 oz. smoked salmon slices
3 slices rye bread
1 tablespoon butter
Lemon twists and dill sprigs to garnish

Filling:
2 oz. cream cheese
1/2 avocado, mashed
2 teaspoons chopped fresh dill
1 small tomato, peeled, seeded, chopped
1/4 teaspoon ground black pepper

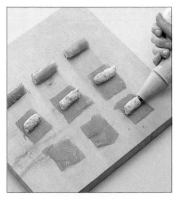

To prepare filling, beat cream cheese in a bowl until soft. Stir avocado into cream cheese until evenly blended. Add dill, chopped tomato and pepper and stir gently. Place in a pastry bag fitted with a 1/2-inch plain nozzle.

Cut smoked salmon in 20 (1-1/2" x 1") rectangles. Pipe a length of cheese mixture across top of short edge of each salmon rectangle and roll up.

Spread rye bread with butter. Cut in 20 rectangles to fit salmon rolls. Place salmon rolls on each piece of bread. Garnish with lemon twists and dill sprigs. Makes 20 pieces.

Filled Button Rarebit

1 cup soft white bread crumbs
1/4 cup chopped ham
1 tablespoon chopped fresh parsley
1 tablespoon fromage frais
24 button mushrooms
4 large slices white bread
2 tablespoons margarine
Celery leaves and parsley to garnish

Topping:
1 tablespoon cider
3/4 cup shredded Cheddar cheese (3 oz.)
1 teaspoon Worcestershire sauce
1/4 teaspoon salt
1/4 teaspoon ground black pepper
1/4 teaspoon dry mustard

Preheat oven to 425F (220C). To prepare filling, mix bread crumbs, ham, parsley and fromage frais in a bowl. Remove stalks from mushrooms, chop finely and stir into filling. Press filling into center of each mushroom. Cut out 24 rounds of bread to match size of mushrooms using a plain cutter. Spread both sides with margarine and place a mushroom on top of each bread round. Arrange on a baking sheet. Bake in oven 5 minutes, then remove.

To prepare topping, place cider in a saucepan. Bring to a boil. Remove saucepan from heat and stir in cheese, Worcestershire sauce, salt, pepper and mustard. Beat well. Spoon a little cheese mixture over top of each filled mushroom. Return to oven and bake 3 to 4 minutes or until cheese has melted and browned slightly. Arrange on a serving dish. Garnish with celery leaves and parsley. Makes 24 pieces.

Olive Cheese Balls

Spiked Cheese Balls

1 cup grated sharp Cheddar cheese, room temperature
3 tablespoons butter, softened
½ cup all-purpose flour
½ teaspoon cayenne pepper
25 to 30 medium-sized pitted or stuffed olives

Preheat oven to 400F (205C). In a bowl cream together cheese and butter. Sift flour with pepper.

4 ounces blue cheese
4 ounces cream cheese
2 tablespoons vodka or Calvados (apple brandy)
2 tablespoons rye bread crumbs
¼ cup butter, softened
3 slices dark, rye bread, crusts removed
1 tablespoon caraway seeds
¼ cup almonds, toasted, finely ground

In a food processor or blender combine blue cheese, cream cheese and butter.

Add flour mixture to creamed mixture. Knead mixture with hands until fairly smooth.

In a small bowl, mix vodka or Calvados with bread crumbs; let stand for 5 minutes. Blend bread crumbs with butter and cheese mixture; chill 30 minutes, or until firm enough to handle.

Cover each olive with a teaspoon of dough. Place on lightly greased cookie sheet. Bake 15 minutes, or until light golden brown. Cool on wire racks. Store in an airtight container in a cool place. Will keep up to 1 week.

Makes 25 to 30.

In a food processor or blender, blend rye bread and caraway seeds into fine crumbs. Roll about 2 teaspoons of cheese mixture into balls; roll half of the balls in rye bread mixture; half in almonds. Refrigerate until firm. Store in the refrigerator up to 1 week.

Each recipe makes about 30.

Flavored Cheeses

Port & Peppercorn Cheese:
1/2 (8-oz.) pkg. Neufchâtel cheese, softened
3/4 cup shredded Cheddar cheese (3 oz.)
2 tablespoons ruby port
Chives and 2 teaspoons pink peppercorns

Combine cheeses and port until evenly blended. Shape in a round ball, then press in a disc shape. Garnish with chives and pink peppercorns.

Blue Cheese:
1/2 (8-oz.) pkg. cream cheese, softened
3/4 cup shredded blue Stilton cheese (3 oz.)
1 teaspoon Dijon-style mustard
1/4 teaspoon cayenne pepper
1/4 cup sunflower seeds
1/4 cup chopped walnuts

Combine cheeses, mustard and cayenne pepper until evenly mixed. Divide mixture in half; mold each half in a cylinder shape. Roll 1 in sunflower seeds and other in walnuts.

Herbed Cheese:
1/2 (8-oz.) pkg. cream cheese
1 small clove garlic, crushed
2 teaspoons snipped chives
1 teaspoon chopped fresh oregano
1 teaspoon chopped fresh thyme
1/4 teaspoon ground black pepper
Bay leaves and 1 teaspoon green peppercorns

Combine 1/3 of cream cheese, garlic, herbs and black pepper until well blended. Shape remaining cheese in a ball and flatten in a thin round. Shape herb mixture in a ball and place in center of cheese round. Press plain cheese over herbed mixture and form in a ball. Garnish with bay leaves and peppercorns.

Refrigerate all cheeses until firm. Use within 10 days. Makes 4 cheeses.

Smoked Trout Pâté

4 oz. thinly sliced smoked lake trout
12 oz. smoked trout fillets
1 cup fresh white bread crumbs
1/2 (8-oz.) pkg. Neufchâtel cheese, softened
1/4 cup unsalted butter, melted
1/2 teaspoon ground black pepper
1 teaspoon finely grated lemon peel
3 tablespoons sherry or brandy
1 tablespoon chopped fresh dill
1 tablespoon chopped fresh tarragon
Lemon twists and dill sprigs to garnish

Line bottom and sides of a 1-lb. loaf pan with plastic wrap.

Trim sliced smoked lake trout to fit bottom and sides of pan. Using a food processor fitted with a metal blade, process trout fillets, bread crumbs, Neufchâtel cheese, butter, pepper, lemon peel, sherry or brandy, dill and tarragon until smooth. Or beat all ingredients in a bowl.

Spoon pâté mixture into prepared pan. Press down firmly and level. Cover top with plastic wrap and refrigerate until firm. Remove plastic wrap. Invert pâté onto a serving plate. Remove remaining plastic wrap and cut in thin slices. Garnish with lemon twists and dill sprigs. Makes 8 servings.

Chili Nuts

2 cups unblanched whole almonds or peanuts
1 tablespoon chili powder
1 large clove garlic, crushed
¼ cup butter, chopped
Kosher salt

In a heavy skillet combine nuts, chili powder, garlic and butter.

Toss over medium heat until nuts become crisp and lightly browned.

Sprinkle with kosher salt and allow to cool. Store in airtight containers.

Makes about 2 cups.

Potted Salmon

½ lb. smoked salmon
1 cup clarified butter
½ teaspoon ground white pepper
Pinch of salt
Fresh chives, to decorate

Blend or process salmon, ¾ cup clarified butter and pepper.

Blend or process to a fine paste. Add salt to taste and refrigerate until firm. Press into small attractive dishes.

Decorate with fresh chives. Melt remaining ¼ cup clarified butter, let cool slightly, spoon over potted salmon, making sure it covers completely. Store in refrigerator up to 1 week.

Makes about 16.

Grand Marnier Pâté

1½ lb. pork livers, cleaned, fibrous membrane removed
½ lb. bacon, cut into pieces
½ cup butter, melted
1 medium-size onion, chopped
¼ cup Grand Marnier (or other orange liqueur)
2 teaspoons grated orange peel
2 tablespoons all-purpose flour
2 eggs, beaten
2 teaspoons salt
1 teaspoon white pepper
½ teaspoon powdered cloves
½ teaspoon powdered allspice
½ teaspoon powdered sage
¼ teaspoon each powdered mace and powdered nutmeg
3 tablespoons whipping cream

Preheat oven to 350F (180C). In a food processor or blender, mix livers, bacon, butter and onion until a smooth purée; add liqueur and orange peel. It may be necessary to do this in batches.

In a bowl, mix together flour, eggs, salt, pepper, cloves, allspice, sage, mace, nutmeg, cream and pureed liver.

Pack into an ungreased 9 x 5-in loaf pan, temire on pâté mold. Put pan into a larger, deep baking dish. Fill larger baking dish with hot water to level of pâté mixture. Bake for 2½ to 3 hours in baking pan. Cool. Remove pâté from larger baking dish and cool in baking pan.

Orange Glaze:
1½ cups clear chicken stock
1½ teaspoons gelatine
2 tablespoons Grand Marnier (or other orange liqueur)
Thin slices of orange, small sprigs of rosemary, celery leaves, black olives and strips of red pepper, for decoration

Orange Glaze:
Warm chicken stock, sprinkle gelatin over surface and stir to dissolve slightly and add Grand Marnier. Decorate pâté with orange slices, small sprigs of rosemary, celery leaves, black olives and strips of red pepper.

Gently spoon the gelatine mixture over pâté a little at a time.

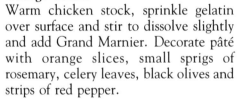

Store in the refrigerator; allow to set 24 hours before using. Will keep up to 1 week well-wrapped.

Makes about 3 lb.

Flavored Oils

Mixed Herb Vinegar

CHILI OIL
6 small or 3 large fresh chilies
2 cups second-grade olive oil, peanut oil or corn oil

GARLIC OIL
5 garlic cloves
1 teaspoon black pepper
2 cups second- grade olive-oil, peanut oil or corn oil

If making chili oil, prick chilies with a fork or point of a small, sharp knife. Slice large chilies. If making garlic oil, peel garlic cloves.

For chili oil, place chilies in a clean bottle. Pour in oil. Seal. Allow to mellow 10 days before using. Will keep up to 2 months.

For garlic oil, place garlic, black pepper and oil in a clean bottle. Seal. Allow to mellow 10 days. Will keep up to 2 weeks.

1 cup chopped mixed fresh herbs such as rosemary, oregano, fennel and basil
2 cups white wine or cider vinegar

In a wide-necked jar that herbs half-fill, place herbs and vinegar. Cover with a vinegar-proof lid. Leave in a warm place for 2 weeks; shake the jar daily.

Strain vinegar through cheesecloth. In a clean 1-pint bottle place a sprig of herbs. Pour in the vinegar. Seal with a vinegar-proof lid.

Variation:
English Herb Vinegar: Use 4 tablespoons chopped fresh sage and 6 tablespoons chopped fresh thyme in place of mixed herbs. Place a sprig of sage and a sprig of thyme in the 1-pint bottle with the strained vinegar.

Tarragon Vinegar: Use 10 tablespoons chopped tarragon in place of mixed herbs. Place a sprig of tarragon in the 1-pint bottle with strained vinegar.

Stuffed Cherry Tomatoes

16 cherry tomatoes, rinsed, patted dry
¾ cup ricotta cheese
8 fresh basil leaves, minced
3 ounces soft blue cheese
¼ cup cottage cheese, sieved
2 tablespoons fresh chopped chives
Ground black pepper
Celery leaves and chive sprigs for decoration

With a sharp knife, cut cap off tomatoes. With a small spoon remove seeds and turn tomatoes upside down onto paper towels to drain.

Beat ricotta cheese until smooth. Stir in basil and add pepper. Blend blue cheese with cottage cheese and chives until smooth. Add pepper.

With a small spoon, pack half the tomatoes with ricotta mixture and half with blue cheese mixture. Cover with caps, garnish with celery leaves and chive sprigs. Chill.

Makes 12 to 16.

Marinated Olives

BLACK CARDAMOM OLIVES
1lb. large black olives in brine
1 orange
1 tablespoon cardamom seeds, crushed
Olive oil

Drain and rinse olives. Peel orange and cut skin (not white pith) into long strips. Place all ingredients into attractive jars and cover with olive oil.

GREEN CORIANDER OLIVES
1lb. large green olives in brine
8 to 10 cloves garlic
2 tablespoons coriander seeds, crushed
2 to 3 sprigs of fresh thyme
Olive oil

Drain and rinse olives. Place all ingredients into jars and cover with olive oil.

Cover and store Black Cardamom Olives and Green Coriander Olives in a cool, dark place. Allow to mellow at least 3 weeks before using.

Each recipe makes 1lb.

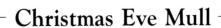

Snowy Flip

4 eggs, separated
1/4 cup superfine sugar
1-1/4 cups whipping cream
2/3 cup milk, chilled
1 cup whiskey or brandy
Soda water
1 teaspoon ground mace
Orange and lemon peel to decorate

Place egg whites and egg yolks into separate bowls. Add 1/2 of sugar to yolks and whisk until pale and creamy. Wash beaters and whisk egg whites until stiff. Add remaining sugar and whisk until stiff.

Add egg whites to yolk mixture and fold in carefully until well mixed and foamy. In a bowl, whip cream until soft peaks form. Fold into egg mixture. Stir in milk and whisky or brandy. Cover with plastic wrap and chill until required.

Stir gently and divide cream mixture among 8 tall glasses. Fill up each with soda water and sprinkle with mace. Decorate with orange and lemon peel. Makes 8 servings.

Christmas Eve Mull

3-1/4 cups white wine
3-1/4 cups red wine
1-1/4 cups sweet red vermouth
1 tablespoon Angostura bitters
6 strips orange peel
8 whole cloves
1 cinnamon stick
8 cardamon pods, crushed
1 tablespoon dark raisins
1/2 cup superfine sugar
Lemon, orange and apple slices

Pour white and red wines into a large stainless steel or enamel saucepan.

Add vermouth, bitters, orange peel, cloves, cinnamon, and cardamon pods. Heat wine mixture gently until very hot but do not boil. Remove saucepan from heat, cover with a lid and cool. Strain wine into a bowl.

Just before serving, return wine to a clean saucepan. Add raisins and sugar. Heat gently until sugar has dissolved and wine is hot enough to drink. Add fruit slices and serve in heatproof mugs. Makes 16 servings.

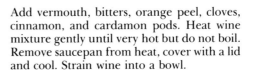

Hot Buttered Rum

4 sticks cinnamon
1 tablespoon plus 1 teaspoon light-brown sugar
1/2 cup dark rum
2-2/3 cups apple cider
2 tablespoons butter
1 teaspoon ground mace
4 lemon slices

Evenly divide cinnamon sticks, brown sugar and rum among 4 warm heatproof glasses or mugs.

In a saucepan, heat apple cider until very hot but not boiling. Fill each glass or mug to top with apple cider.

Add a dot of butter to each. Sprinkle with mace and add a lemon slice. Stir well and serve. Makes 4 servings.

Apples & Ale Mull

2 lb. cooking apples
5 cups ginger ale or ginger beer
6 whole cloves
1 blade mace
1 teaspoon grated nutmeg
1/2 teaspoon ground ginger
3 strips orange peel
Red and green apple and lemon slices

Preheat oven to 400F (205C). Wash apples and remove stalks. Arrange on a baking sheet and bake in oven 30 to 40 minutes or until soft.

Place apples in a saucepan and mash to break up apples. Add ginger ale or ginger beer, cloves, mace, ginger and orange peel. Bring to a boil. Remove from heat and cool. Strain apple mixture through a nylon sieve into a bowl, pressing through as much apple as possible.

Just before serving, return apple and ale mixture to a clean saucepan. Heat until hot enough to drink. Float apple and lemon slices on top and serve in heatproof glasses or mugs. Makes 10 servings.

Snowball Fizz

4 (1-oz.) squares white chocolate
Finely grated peel and juice 2 limes
1-1/2 cups red or white grape juice
1 egg white
1 tablespoon plus 2 teaspoons superfine sugar
Soda or sparkling water
1 teaspoon grated milk chocolate
4 drinking straws
4 cocktail umbrellas, if desired

Break up white chocolate. Place in bowl set over a saucepan of hand-hot water. Stir occasionally until melted and smooth. Stir in lime peel and juice until well blended.

Divide grape juice equally among 4 glasses. Add 1/4 of chocolate-lime mixture to each and stir until well blended.

In a bowl, whisk egg white until stiff. Add sugar a little at a time and whisk until thick. Just before serving, divide meringue among glasses and fill to top with soda or sparkling water. Sprinkle with milk chocolate and serve with drinking straws and cocktail umbrellas, if desired. Makes 4 servings.

Rosé Glow

1/4 cup sweet red vermouth
1/4 cup cherry brandy liqueur
1/4 cup brandy
1 kiwifruit, peeled, sliced
8 maraschino cherries, halved
Orange, lemon and lime slices
1 bottle rosé wine
Ice cubes
Mint and borage sprigs
Rose petals, if desired
1 bottle sparkling white wine

In a large punch bowl, pour vermouth, cherry brandy and brandy. Add kiwifruit, cherries and citrus fruit slices. Stir to mix well.

Just before serving, pour in rosé wine. Add ice cubes, mint and borage sprigs and rose petals, if desired.

At the last minute, add sparkling wine and serve in punch glasses or cups, including some fruit and ice. Makes 10 servings.

LUNCHES & DINNERS

Roast Stuffed Turkey

1 (8-lb.) oven-ready turkey with giblets
2-1/2 cups water

Stuffing:
4-1/4 cups soft white bread crumbs
1 large onion, finely chopped
3 celery stalks, finely chopped
Finely grated peel and juice 1 lemon
8 plums, pitted, chopped
2/3 cup red wine
2 cups chestnut puree
1 tablespoon chopped fresh sage
1 tablespoon chopped fresh thyme
1 tablespoon chopped fresh oregano
Salt and pepper to taste
1 lb. bacon
1/2 cup all-purpose flour

Remove giblets from turkey. Place in a saucepan with water. Bring to boil, cover and simmer 1 hour. Strain stock into a bowl; reserve liver. To prepare stuffing, place bread crumbs, onion, celery, lemon peel and juice, plums and wine in a saucepan. Bring to a boil, stirring constantly, and cook 1 minute. In a food processor fitted with a metal blade, process turkey liver, chestnut puree and herbs until smooth. Season with salt and pepper. Add bread crumb mixture and process until evenly blended.

Place 1/3 of stuffing into neck end of turkey. Pull over flap of skin and secure under turkey with skewers or string. Fill cavity of turkey with remaining stuffing. Pull skin over nose and secure with skewers or string. Truss turkey with string, securing wings and legs closely to body, and place in a roasting pan.

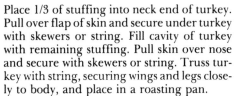

Preheat oven to 375F (190C). Cover whole turkey with strips of bacon over breast bone, body, legs and wings to keep moist during cooking.

Bake turkey in oven 2 hours. Remove bacon and cover turkey and pan with thick foil. Return to oven another 1 to 1-1/2 hours or until turkey is tender and only clear juices run when pierced with a knife between legs of turkey. Let stand in pan 20 minutes before removing. Remove any skewers or trussing string and place on a warmed serving dish. Chop crispy bacon finely.

To prepare gravy, blend flour and some stock until smooth. Strain stock into a saucepan and stir in flour mixture. Bring to a boil, stirring until thickened. Cook 2 minutes. Taste and season with salt and pepper and pour into a gravy boat. Serve turkey with bread stuffing and chopped bacon. Makes 10 servings.

Apple & Pickled Walnut Stuffing

2 tablespoons butter
4 shallots, chopped
1 lb. cooking apples, grated
Finely grated peel and juice 1 lemon
2 cups soft white bread crumbs
2 tablespoons chopped fresh thyme
1/2 teaspoon salt
1/2 teaspoon ground black pepper
1/2 cup chopped walnuts
5 pickled walnuts, sliced
1 egg, beaten

Melt butter in a saucepan. Add shallots, apples and lemon peel and juice. Cook over moderate heat, stirring occasionally, until onion and apple are tender. Remove saucepan from heat.

In a bowl, mix bread crumbs, thyme, salt, pepper and chopped and pickled walnuts.

Add apple mixture and beaten egg to bread crumb mixture. Stir well until evenly blended. Makes 5 cups.

Note
This recipe makes enough stuffing for a 5- to 6-lb. goose. Cut recipe in half for a duck or double recipe for a turkey.

Cranberry & Orange Stuffing

2 cups cranberries
Grated peel and juice 2 oranges
3 tablespoons honey
2 tablespoons butter
2 onions, chopped
1 teaspoon salt
1/2 teaspoon ground black pepper
1/2 teaspoon cayenne pepper
1 teaspoon ground mace
1 tablespoon plus 1 teaspoon chopped fresh
   sage
4-1/4 cups soft white bread crumbs
1/2 cup pine nuts

In a saucepan, combine cranberries and orange peel and juice. Bring to a boil. Cover and simmer very gently 1 minute or until cranberries are just tender. Remove saucepan from heat. Stir in honey. Pour cranberries into a bowl.

Melt butter in saucepan. Stir in onions and cook gently 2 minutes until tender. Add salt, pepper, cayenne, mace and sage and mix until well blended.

Stir onion mixture, bread crumbs and pine nuts into cranberries until well mixed. Makes 6 cups.

Note
This recipe makes enough stuffing for an 8-pound turkey. Cut recipe in half for a duck.

Gooseberry Goose

1 (8-lb.) oven-ready goose
2 tablespoons butter
6 shallots, finely chopped
6-1/4 cups soft bread crumbs
2/3 cup gooseberry juice
1-1/4 cups freshly chopped mixed herbs, such
    as marjoram, basil, thyme, rosemary, parsley
1 teaspoon salt
1 teaspoon ground black pepper
12 slices bacon
1 tablespoon Dijon-style mustard
1 cup elderflower wine
1 lb. gooseberries, cooked
1 tablespoon arrowroot
1 tablespoon plus 2 teaspoons superfine sugar
1/4 cup elderberries, if desired

Preheat oven to 425F (220C). Chop goose giblets and reserve liver. Use giblets to prepare stock. Pierce skin of goose. To prepare stuffing, melt butter. Add goose liver and shallots and fry 2 minutes. Reserve 2 tablespoons of bread crumbs. Stir in 1/2 of gooseberry juice, herbs, remaining bread crumbs, salt and pepper until well mixed. Stuff neck end and body cavity of goose. In a roasting pan, cover goose with bacon and bake 45 minutes. Reduce oven to 375F (190C) and bake 1-1/2 hours, pouring off fat during baking.

Chop bacon very finely. Mix bacon and remaining bread crumbs. Brush goose with mustard and sprinkle with bread crumb mixture. Bake another 20 to 30 minutes or until meat is tender. Place on a serving plate. Pour away fat. To prepare sauce, add 1/4 cup of stock to roasting pan and mix with remaining gooseberry juice, wine, gooseberries, arrowroot and sugar. Bring to a boil, stirring constantly and cook 1 minute. In a food processor, process sauce until smooth. Strain and stir in elderberries, if desired. Serve sauce with goose. Makes 8 servings.

Spiced Honey Ham

1 (3-lb.) smoked ham
Finely shredded peel and juice 2 oranges
2 tablespoons honey
1 teaspoon ground mace
1 teaspoon freshly grated ginger
4 oz. kumquats, sliced
2 tablespoons whole cloves
3/4 cup water
1 tablespoon cornstarch

Soak ham in a bowl of cold water overnight. Drain and transfer to a large saucepan. Cover with fresh cold water. Bring to a boil, cover and cook 30 minutes. Drain and cool. Remove skin from ham, leaving a layer of fat on surface of ham. Score fat in a lattice pattern with a sharp knife.

Preheat oven to 375F (190C). Place ham in a roasting pan. In a bowl, mix orange peel and juice, honey, mace and ginger until evenly blended. Brush surface of ham and bake in oven 30 minutes. Remove ham from oven and brush surface with more orange mixture.

Stud surface of ham with kumquat slices; hold in position with whole cloves. Return to oven another 30 to 40 minutes or until ham is golden brown and tender. Remove and place on a serving dish. Keep warm. To prepare sauce, add water to roasting pan. Stir to mix juices, then strain into a saucepan. Blend cornstarch with remaining orange juice and honey mixture. Add to pan, bring to a boil and cook 1 minute. Serve ham with sauce. Makes 8 servings.

Party Terrine

1 lb. pork, boned
1 lb. bacon
4 (4-oz.) boneless chicken breast fillets
1 lb. boneless veal
2/3 cup white wine
2 tablespoons Madeira wine
2 tablespoons chicken stock
2 teaspoons salt
1-1/2 teaspoons ground black pepper
10 juniper berries, crushed
2 cloves garlic, crushed
6 bay leaves
Additional bay leaves, orange twists and
    cranberries to garnish
Toast triangles, if desired

Preheat oven to 300F (150C). Using a mincer fitted with a fine blade or a food processor fitted with a metal blade, mince pork, bacon, chicken and veal. In a large bowl, combine meats, wines, chicken stock, salt, pepper, juniper berries and garlic. Mix together until thoroughly blended. Spoon mixture into a 7-1/2-cup ovenproof dish.

Press down firmly and arrange 6 bay leaves on top. Cover dish with a double thickness of foil. Stand dish in a pan half-filled with cold water. Bake in oven 1-3/4 to 2 hours or until terrine feels firm in center and shrinks from side of dish. Let stand until completely cold in dish. Garnish with additional bay leaves, orange twists and cranberries. Serve with toast triangles, if desired. Makes 20 servings.

Game Hens Noel

2 large game hens
4 slices bacon
1 tablespoon all-purpose flour
2/3 cup white wine
Chicken stock

Stuffing:
1 tablespoon butter
1 shallot, finely chopped
8 dried apricots, chopped
2 tablespoons corn kernels
1 tablespoon fresh chopped mixed sage, thyme
    and parsley
1/4 cup white wine
1/2 teaspoon salt
1/2 teaspoon ground black pepper

Preheat oven to 375F (190C). Place game hens into a small roasting pan. To prepare stuffing, melt butter in a saucepan. Add shallot and cook until tender, stirring occasionally. Remove saucepan from heat. Stir in apricots, corn, herbs, wine, salt and pepper. Stir until evenly mixed. Stuff game hens with stuffing; place in a roasting pan.

Cover breasts and bodies of game hens with strips of bacon. Bake 1 hour or until meat is tender. Remove bacon, chop finely and sprinkle over each game hen. Stir flour into juices in roasting pan and add wine. Bring to a boil, stirring constantly. Add some stock, if necessary, to dilute gravy. Cook 2 minutes. Serve sauce on game hens. Makes 2 servings.

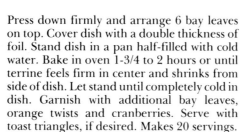

Turkey Vegetable Strudel

9 leaves phyllo or strudel pastry, thawed
1/2 cup plus 3 tablespoons butter
1/4 cup all-purpose flour
1 bay leaf
1 cup milk
2/3 cup half and half
1/2 teaspoon salt
1/2 teaspoon ground black pepper
3/4 cup sliced leek
3/4 cup thinly sliced fennel
1 cup sliced button mushrooms
2/3 cup corn kernels
1 tablespoon plus 1 teaspoon chopped fresh
    parsley
1 cup diced cooked turkey

Cover phyllo pastry with a damp cloth to prevent drying. To prepare filling, combine 3 tablespoons of butter, flour, bay leaf and milk in a saucepan. Bring to a boil, whisking until thick. Cook gently 2 minutes. Stir in half and half, salt and pepper. Place 2 tablespoons of butter in a large skillet. Fry leek, fennel and mushrooms gently 2 to 3 minutes or until tender. Stir in corn, parsley and turkey. Let stand until cold. Combine thickened milk mixture and turkey mixture.

Preheat oven to 425F (220C). Line a baking sheet with parchment paper. Melt remaining butter. Lay 3 sheets of phyllo pastry flat on a tea towel, brushing in between each sheet with melted butter. Spread with 1/3 of filling to within 1/2 inch of edges; repeat twice more using pastry and filling. Fold in all edges and roll up in a roll with aid of tea towel and roll onto a prepared baking sheet. Brush with remaining butter. Bake in oven 20 to 25 minutes or until golden brown. Cut in slices and serve. Makes 6 servings.

Fruit Pork Pillows

2 tablespoons butter
2 (1-lb.) pork tenderloins, cut in 4 pieces each
3 tablespoons whipping cream, whipped
1 cup chopped dried apricots
1 lb. puff pastry, thawed
2/3 cup sweet cherries, pitted, halved
Fresh sage leaves
Salt and ground black pepper to taste
1 egg, beaten

Preheat oven to 400F (205C). Line a baking sheet with waxed paper. Melt butter in a large skillet. Fry pork pieces quickly 1 minute, turning once, to seal. Drain on paper towels and cool.

In a bowl, whip cream until thick. Fold in apricots. Cut pastry in 8 pieces. Roll out 1 piece very thinly and trim to a square. Spread 1/8 of apricot filling over center. Top with 4 cherry halves, 1 sage leaf and a piece of pork. Season with salt and pepper.

Brush pastry edges with beaten egg; fold pastry over pork and seal well. Invert onto prepared baking sheet and brush with egg. Repeat to make another 7 pillows. Roll out and cut trimmings in holly leaves and berries and decorate each pillow. Brush with egg. Bake in oven 20 to 30 minutes or until pastry has risen and is golden brown. Garnish with remaining cherries and sage leaves and serve hot. Makes 8 servings.

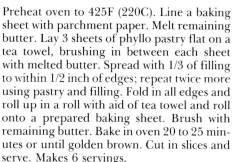

Hot Malt Whiskey Mustard

¼ cup black mustard seeds
¼ cup white mustard seeds
4 tablespoons water
⅔ cup cider vinegar
⅔ cup whiskey
½ cup honey
1 tablespoon ground nutmeg
1 tablespoon salt
Add if a very grainy mustard is desired:
  ¼ cup black mustard seeds
  ¼ cup white mustard seeds

In a blender grind black and white mustard seeds.

In a glass or ceramic bowl mix together mustard powder and water; let stand 30 minutes.

Place mustard mixture, vinegar, whiskey, honey, nutmeg and salt in blender or food processor. Process until mustard acquires a grainy texture. Add more honey if ingredients look too dry. Add additional whole black and white mustard seeds if desired. Blend again, breaking down grains but still retaining a 'whole grain' appearance. Cover; let stand overnight. Moisten with more honey if mixture appears too dry. Pour into sterilized jars and seal. Store in a cool, dark place – allow to mellow 3 weeks before using. Refrigerate after opening.

Makes 2½ to 3 cups.

Herb Butters

BASIL BUTTER

½ cup butter, softened
8 to 10 fresh basil leaves, minced

Beat butter and basil together until creamy. Press into a butter mold or roll into a cylinder and cover in plastic wrap. Chill until firm.

MIXED HERB BUTTER

1 cup butter, softened
1 teaspoon each of finely chopped fresh parsley, sage, oregano and rosemary

Beat butter until creamy. Add the herbs and beat again. Roll into cylinders and cover with plastic wrap, baking parchment or wax paper. Refrigerate until firm.

GARLIC BUTTER

½ cup butter
4 cloves garlic, crushed
½ teaspoon white pepper
2 tablespoons finely chopped fresh parsley

Beat butter, garlic, pepper and parsley together until creamy. Press into a butter mold. Refrigerate until firm.

Turkey Risotto

1/4 cup butter
1 large onion, sliced
1 clove garlic, crushed
4 oz. button mushrooms, sliced
1 cup Italian risotto rice
1 teaspoon saffron strands
1 teaspoon salt
1/2 teaspoon ground black pepper
1-3/4 cups turkey stock
2/3 cup white wine
1 small red bell pepper
1 small yellow bell pepper
10 oz. cooked turkey
2 tablespoons shredded Gruyere cheese
1 tablespoon chopped fresh parsley
Small red and yellow bell pepper rings and
     parsley to garnish

Melt butter in a saucepan. Add onion, garlic and mushrooms and cook 2 minutes or until tender. Stir in rice and cook another 2 minutes. Add saffron, salt, pepper, stock and wine. Bring to a boil, stirring constantly, then cover and cook very gently 15 minutes. Broil peppers until skin is charred and peppers are tender. Remove stalk, seeds and skin and cut peppers in fine strips. Cut turkey in bite-sized pieces.

Add turkey and peppers to risotto. Stir carefully to distribute ingredients. Cover and cook another 5 minutes or until rice is tender and mixture is creamy but not dry. Arrange on a warmed serving plate. Sprinkle with cheese and parsley. Garnish with bell pepper rings and parsley and serve hot. Makes 4 to 6 servings.

Turkey Soup

1 turkey, chicken or goose carcass
1/3 cup butter
3 slices bacon, chopped
1 onion, chopped
2 carrots, chopped
3 stalks celery, chopped
2 leeks, sliced
Cold water
1/4 to 1/2 cup all-purpose flour
1 teaspoon salt
1 teaspoon ground black pepper
2/3 cup sherry or wine
Croutons and chopped parsley to garnish

Preheat oven to 425F (220C). Break up carcass in pieces, reserving any pieces of meat. Place carcass in a roasting pan with skin or any leftover bones. Bake 45 to 50 minutes or until bones are golden brown.

Melt 2 tablespoons of butter in a large saucepan. Add bacon, onion, carrots, celery and leeks. Fry quickly until vegetables are lightly browned, stirring frequently. Add carcass and cover with enough cold water to cover all ingredients. Bring to a boil. Cover and simmer 2 to 3 hours.

Strain stock into a large bowl. Cool overnight. Remove fat from top. Melt remaining butter in a saucepan. Stir in flour and cook 1 minute, stirring constantly. Gradually add stock. Bring to a boil, stirring constantly, and cook 5 minutes. Add reserved turkey meat, salt, pepper and sherry or wine. Garnish with croutons and chopped parsley and serve hot. Makes 6 servings.

Red Currant & Clementine Duck

1 (5-lb.) oven-ready duck
Salt
2 tablespoons butter
3 shallots, finely chopped
1-1/4 cups rosé wine
1/2 teaspoon salt
1/2 teaspoon ground black pepper
1 teaspoon whole-grain mustard
1 tablespoon chopped fresh oregano
Finely grated peel and juice 2 clementines
2 tablespoons red currant jelly
3/4 cup red currants, thawed
1 egg, beaten
1-1/2 cups fresh white bread crumbs

Preheat oven to 425F (220C). Remove giblets from duck. Chop liver and reserve. Prepare stock with remainder. Pierce skin all over with a fork; rub salt into skin. Place duck in a roasting pan. Bake in oven 1 hour or until golden brown. Remove and cool 15 minutes. Strain fat from roasting pan. Meanwhile, melt butter in a saucepan. Fry reserved liver and shallots quickly, stirring constantly, until shallots are tender. Stir in wine, salt, pepper and mustard. Bring to a boil and cook 5 minutes. Pour mixture into a roasting pan. Mix with juices and strain back into saucepan. Stir in oregano, clementine peel and juice and red currant jelly.

Using a sharp knife, cut off legs and wings from duck. Slice breast in thin slices and arrange in a warm ovenproof dish. Pour over sauce and red currants. Cover dish with lid or foil. Brush legs and wings with egg; coat each in bread crumbs and arrange in roasting pan. Return to oven 20 to 30 minutes or until crisp and golden brown. Arrange in dish with breast meat and sauce. Makes 4 servings.

Vegetable-Turkey Kebabs

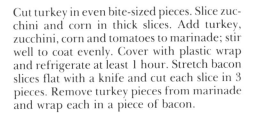

8 oz. cooked turkey breast
3 small zucchini
1 ear of corn, thawed if frozen
8 cherry tomatoes
8 slices bacon
Hot cooked pasta, if desired
Rosemary sprigs to garnish

Marinade:
2 tablespoons almond oil
1/2 teaspoon salt
1/2 teaspoon ground black pepper
1 teaspoon Dijon-style mustard
2 teaspoons honey
1 tablespoon chopped fresh rosemary
1 tablespoon raspberry vinegar

To prepare marinade, in a bowl, place almond oil, salt, pepper, mustard, honey, rosemary and vinegar. Beat well to blend.

Cut turkey in even bite-sized pieces. Slice zucchini and corn in thick slices. Add turkey, zucchini, corn and tomatoes to marinade; stir well to coat evenly. Cover with plastic wrap and refrigerate at least 1 hour. Stretch bacon slices flat with a knife and cut each slice in 3 pieces. Remove turkey pieces from marinade and wrap each in a piece of bacon.

Using 4 long wooden skewers, thread a mixture of ingredients onto each. Brush well with marinade and arrange on a grill pan lined with foil. Broil under a hot grill for 5 to 6 minutes, turning frequently, or until bacon is crisp and vegetables are just tender. Serve immediately on hot cooked pasta, if desired. Garnish with rosemary. Makes 4 servings.

Broccoli & Cauliflower Crumble

8 oz. cauliflower florets
8 oz. broccoli florets
Hard-cooked egg wedges and parsley sprigs to
  garnish

Topping:
2 tablespoons butter
1 cup soft white bread crumbs
1 tablespoon chopped fresh parsley
1 hard-cooked egg, sieved

Sauce:
2 tablespoons butter
1/4 cup all-purpose flour
1-1/4 cups milk
1/2 teaspoon salt
1/2 teaspoon ground black pepper

To prepare topping, heat butter in a skillet.
Add bread crumbs and fry until golden
brown and crisp. In a bowl, combine bread
crumbs, parsley and sieved egg.

To prepare sauce, place butter, flour, milk,
salt and pepper in a saucepan. Whisk over
moderate heat until thick. Cook 1 to 2 minutes. Keep warm.

In a saucepan, cook cauliflower and broccoli
in boiling salted water 3 to 4 minutes or until
just tender. Drain and place in a warmed serving dish. Pour over sauce and sprinkle with
topping. Garnish with egg wedges and parsley sprigs. Makes 4 to 6 servings.

Brussel Sprouts with Almonds

1 lb. small Brussel sprouts
2 tablespoons butter
1/4 cup flaked almonds
1 clove garlic, crushed
1 teaspoon grated lemon peel
1 teaspoon fresh lemon juice
1/2 teaspoon salt
1/2 teaspoon ground black pepper
Lemon twists and herb sprigs to garnish

Trim tops off sprouts and cut across top of
each. In a saucepan, cook sprouts in boiling
salted water 4 to 5 minutes or until just tender. Drain well and place in a warmed serving
dish.

Meanwhile, melt butter in a skillet. Add
flaked almonds and garlic. Fry until almonds
are golden brown. Stir in lemon peel, juice,
salt and pepper and mix well.

Sprinkle almonds over sprouts; stir gently to
mix. Garnish with lemon twists and herb
sprigs. Makes 4 servings.

Soufflé Potatoes

4 large potatoes
2 tablespoons butter
2 tablespoons half and half
1 teaspoon salt
1/2 teaspoon ground black pepper
1/2 teaspoon grated nutmeg
2 eggs, separated
Parsley sprigs to garnish

Preheat oven to 425F (220C). Scrub potatoes until skins are clean and remove any 'eyes.' Using a small sharp knife, pierce each potato several times and arrange on a baking sheet. Bake in oven 1 hour or until potatoes are tender.

Cut each potato in half. Carefully scoop out potato flesh and place in a bowl. Replace potato skins on baking sheet and bake 10 to 15 minutes or until crisp and golden. Meanwhile, mash or beat potato flesh until smooth. Add butter, half and half, salt, pepper, nutmeg and egg yolks. Mash or beat until thoroughly blended.

In a small bowl, stiffly whisk egg whites until stiff. Using a spatula, gently fold egg whites into potato mixture until evenly mixed. Fill each potato skin with mixture and bake 10 to 15 minutes or until risen and lightly browned. Garnish with parsley sprigs and serve immediately. Makes 8 servings.

Variation:
Add 1/2 cup chopped crispy bacon, shredded cheese or chopped mixed fresh herbs to potato mixture.

Creamed Spinach & Celery

2 lb. fresh spinach
6 stalks celery
2 tablespoons butter
1 teaspoon grated nutmeg
1/3 cup whipping cream
1/4 teaspoon salt
1/2 teaspoon ground black pepper
Additional celery slices and leaves to garnish

Stem and wash spinach. Wash and thinly slice celery. In 2 saucepans, cook celery and spinach separately in boiling salted water until just tender. Drain thoroughly. Press excess water from spinach.

Line bottom and sides of 8 warm individual soufflé dishes with whole spinach leaves. Coarsely chop remaining spinach. Melt butter in a saucepan. Add nutmeg, whipping cream, salt and pepper and bring to a boil. Add chopped spinach and toss well.

Half-fill each soufflé dish with spinach mixture and cover each with a layer of celery. Fill each to top with remaining chopped spinach. Press firmly. Invert spinach molds to serve. Garnish with celery slices and leaves. Makes 8 servings.

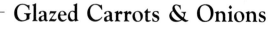

Baked Potato Layer

2 lb. medium-size potatoes
2 tablespoons butter
1 clove garlic, crushed
1 teaspoon salt
1 teaspoon ground black pepper
1 cup shredded Cheddar cheese (4 oz.)
1-1/4 cups milk
2/3 cup half and half
1 large egg, beaten
Parsley sprigs to garnish

Preheat oven to 375F (190C). Using a sharp knife, peel and very thinly slice potatoes or use a food processor fitted with a fine slicing blade. Lightly butter a 9-inch shallow oven-proof dish using 1/2 of butter.

Arrange a layer of potato slices over bottom and up sides of dish. Sprinkle with some of garlic, salt, pepper and cheese. Continue to layer until all these ingredients have been used, finishing with a layer of potatoes and a sprinkling of cheese.

In a bowl, whisk milk, half and half and egg until smooth. Pour over potato layer and dot with remaining butter. Bake 1 hour or until golden brown and potatoes are tender. Garnish with parsley sprigs and serve hot. Makes 4 servings.

Glazed Carrots & Onions

12 small even-sized carrots
16 pickling onions
1 teaspoon salt
1/4 cup turkey or chicken stock
1 tablespoon superfine sugar
2 tablespoons butter
1 tablespoon chopped fresh parsley
Herb sprigs to garnish

Peel and trim carrots so they are all even in size. Peel and trim onions. In 2 saucepans, cook carrots and onions separately in boiling salted water 5 to 8 minutes or until just tender. Drain well.

In a medium saucepan, combine stock, sugar and butter. Heat gently, stirring until sugar has dissolved and butter has melted. Boil rapidly until mixture is reduced by half.

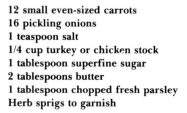

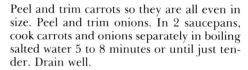

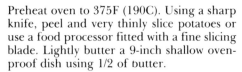

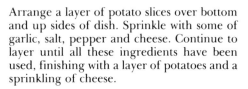

Add carrots, onions and parsley. Toss well in glaze and arrange on a warmed serving dish. Garnish with herb sprigs. Makes 4 servings.

PUDDINGS, DESSERTS, & CAKES

Round Christmas Pudding

3 cups mixed dried fruit
1/2 cup chopped prunes
1/3 cup chopped glacé cherries
1/2 cup chopped almonds
1/4 cup grated carrot
1/4 cup grated cooking apple
Finely grated peel and juice 1 orange
1 tablespoon molasses
1 tablespoon brandy
1/3 cup stout
1 egg, beaten
1/4 cup butter, melted
1/3 cup dark-brown sugar
3/4 teaspoon ground allspice
1/2 cup all-purpose flour
1 cup soft white bread crumbs
Holly sprigs to decorate
Additional brandy
1 recipe Brandy Butter, opposite page

Combine mixed fruit, prunes, cherries, almonds, carrot, apple, orange peel and juice, molasses, brandy and stout. Stir in egg, butter, brown sugar, allspice, flour and bread crumbs. Cover with plastic wrap and refrigerate.

Using a 5-inch buttered spherical mold or a rice steamer mold lined with a double thickness of foil, fill each half of mold with mixture. Place 2 halves together, securing mold tightly.

Half-fill a saucepan with water. Bring to a boil and place mold in so water comes just below seam of mold. Cover and simmer 6 hours. Cool in mold, then turn out. When cold, wrap in foil. To reheat, unwrap and replace in mold. Cook as before in simmering water 2 to 3 hours. Decorate with holly. Warm brandy, spoon over pudding and light. Serve with Brandy Butter. Makes 8 servings.

Brandy Butter

1 cup unsalted butter
1 cup superfine sugar
1/3 cup brandy
Holly sprig to decorate

In a bowl or food processor fitted with a metal blade, beat or process butter until white and creamy. Add sugar and beat or process until light and fluffy.

Add brandy a drop at a time, beating continuously, until enough has been added to well-flavor butter. Take care mixture does not curdle through overbeating.

Spoon butter into a glass dish and serve with a spoon or spread about 1/2 inch thick over a flat dish and chill until hard. Using a fancy cutter, cut in shapes and arrange on a chilled serving dish. Decorate with holly. Makes 8 servings.

Ginger Marron Glacé

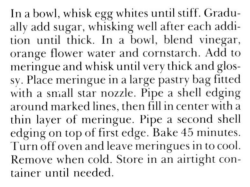

Pavlova:
3 egg whites
1 cup superfine sugar
1 teaspoon white vinegar
1 teaspoon orange flower water
1 teaspoon cornstach
Mint sprigs to decorate

Filling:
1-1/4 cups whipping cream
3 pieces preserved stem ginger in syrup,
  chopped
10 whole marrons glacés, cut in pieces
Vanilla ice cream

Preheat oven to 275F (135C). Line 2 baking sheets with parchment paper. Mark 10 (3-inch) circles and invert paper.

In a bowl, whisk egg whites until stiff. Gradually add sugar, whisking well after each addition until thick. In a bowl, blend vinegar, orange flower water and cornstarch. Add to meringue and whisk until very thick and glossy. Place meringue in a large pastry bag fitted with a small star nozzle. Pipe a shell edging around marked lines, then fill in center with a thin layer of meringue. Pipe a second shell edging on top of first edge. Bake 45 minutes. Turn off oven and leave meringues in to cool. Remove when cold. Store in an airtight container until needed.

In a bowl, whip cream until thick. Place 1/2 of whipped cream into pastry bag fitted with a nozzle. Fold chopped ginger into remaining whipped cream and spoon into center of each meringue. Just before serving, top each with balls of ice cream and a marron glacé. Decorate with mint sprigs. Makes 10 servings.

Soufflé Lime & Chocolate Layer

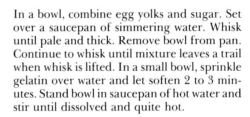

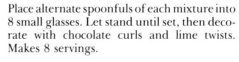

4 eggs, separated
1/3 cup superfine sugar
1 tablespoon plain gelatin
3 tablespoons water
Finely grated peel and juice 1 lime
2 (1-oz.) squares semi-sweet chocolate, melted
1-1/4 cups whipping cream
Chocolate curls and lime peel to decorate

In a bowl, combine egg yolks and sugar. Set over a saucepan of simmering water. Whisk until pale and thick. Remove bowl from pan. Continue to whisk until mixture leaves a trail when whisk is lifted. In a small bowl, sprinkle gelatin over water and let soften 2 to 3 minutes. Stand bowl in saucepan of hot water and stir until dissolved and quite hot.

Stir gelatin into egg yolk mixture until well blended. Pour 1/2 of mixture into another bowl. Stir grated lime peel and juice into 1 mixture and chocolate into remaining mixture until well blended. In a small bowl, whisk egg whites until stiff. In another small bowl, whip cream until thick. Add 1/2 of egg whites and cream to each mixture and fold in carefully until evenly blended.

Place alternate spoonfuls of each mixture into 8 small glasses. Let stand until set, then decorate with chocolate curls and lime twists. Makes 8 servings.

Rose Custard Creams

1-1/4 cups milk
1-1/4 cups whipping cream
2 eggs
2 egg yolks
2 tablespoons plus 2 teaspoons superfine sugar
2 tablespoons plus 2 teaspoons rosé water

Marinated Fruit:
1 tablespoon plus 1 teaspoon rose water
1 tablespoon plus 1 teaspoon rosé wine
2 tablespoons plus 2 teaspoons powdered sugar
Petals from 2 scented roses
1 cup strawberries, sliced
1 cup raspberries, thawed if frozen
1 starfruit, sliced

Preheat oven to 300F (150C). In a saucepan, bring milk and whipping cream almost to boiling point.

In a bowl, beat eggs and egg yolks. Pour milk mixture into eggs, stirring well. Add sugar and rose water and stir until well blended. Divide mixture among 8 individual soufflé dishes. Stand dishes in a roasting pan and half-fill pan with cold water. Bake in oven about 1 hour or until custard has set. Remove dishes from water and refrigerate until cold.

To prepare marinated fruit, mix rose water, wine, powdered sugar and rose petals in a bowl. Add fruit; stir until well mixed. Cover with plastic wrap and chill until ready to serve. Turn custards out onto individual plates and serve with marinated fruit. Makes 8 servings.

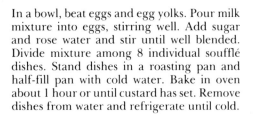

Tipsy Fruit Jelly

3 lemons
1-1/4 cups water
1/2 cup superfine sugar
2/3 cup claret
2 tablespoons plain gelatin
1/4 cup hot water
12 oz. mixed fresh fruit such as grapes, lychees, pineapple, clementines, cut up
Additional fresh fruit and whipped cream to decorate

Using a vegetable peeler or sharp knife, pare peel from lemons. Squeeze juice. In a saucepan, combine peel and water and bring to a boil. Add sugar; stir until dissolved. Let stand until cold, then strain. Stir in lemon juice. Pour 1/3 of lemon mixture into a bowl. Add claret, stir until blended.

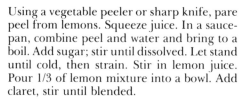

In a small bowl, sprinkle gelatin over hot water. Let stand until softened. Place bowl in a saucepan of hot water. Stir until dissolved and quite hot. Add 1/2 of gelatin to claret mixture, stirring well, and the remainder to lemon mixture, stirring well. Halve grapes and lychees, remove seeds and pits. Peel and slice pineapple and clementines.

Arrange 1/4 of mixed fruit in bottom of 6 individual molds. Spoon enough lemon jelly over fruit to cover. Refrigerate until set. Arrange a second layer of fruit over set jelly layer and cover with claret jelly; refrigerate until set. Repeat to make another lemon fruit layer and claret fruit layer. Refrigerate until firmly set. Remove from molds by dipping into hand-hot water and invert onto a plate. Decorate with fresh fruit and piped whipped cream. Makes 6 servings.

Amaretti Cheese Whip

1/4 cup superfine sugar
2 eggs, separated
1-1/4 cups mascarpone cream cheese, beaten
Finely grated peel 1 tangerine
3/4 cup chopped mixed glacé fruits
1/4 cup broken Amaretti cookies (macaroons)
1 tablespoon plus 1 teaspoon Amaretto liqueur
2/3 cup whipping cream

Decoration:
Glacé fruits and Amaretti cookies (macaroons)
    to decorate

In a bowl, combine sugar and egg yolks. Set over a saucepan of simmering water. Whisk until mixture leaves a trail when whisk is lifted.

Stir in cream cheese, tangerine peel, chopped glacé fruits, broken Amaretti cookies and liqueur. In a small bowl, whisk egg whites until stiff. In another small bowl, whip whipping cream until thick. Add egg whites and whipped cream to cream cheese mixture and fold in carefully until mixture is evenly blended. Cover with plastic wrap and chill until needed.

Just before serving, divide mixture among 6 to 8 small dishes. Decorate with glacé fruit and Amaretti cookies. Makes 6 to 8 servings.

Lychee & Port Ice Cream

1/2 cup superfine sugar
2/3 cup ruby port
20 fresh lychees or 1 (15-oz.) can lychees
1 tablespoon plus 1 teaspoon lime juice
1-1/4 cups whipping cream
Fresh or canned lychees and lime peel twists to
    decorate

In a saucepan, combine sugar and port. Heat gently, stirring occasionally, until sugar has dissolved. Peel lychees and remove pits or drain canned lychees. Add lychees to port mixture. Bring to a boil, cover and cook very gently 2 minutes. Let stand until completely cold.

Using a food processor fitted with a metal blade, process port and lychees until smooth. Pour mixture into a sieve set over a bowl and rub mixture through using a wooden spoon. Stir in lime juice. In a bowl, whip cream until thick. Add port mixture to whipped cream and fold in until evenly blended. Pour mixture into a plastic container, cover and freeze 1 to 2 hours or until mixture is almost frozen but still soft.

Return mixture to food processor. Process until smooth and creamy. Return mixture to plastic container and freeze until firm. Scoop ice cream to serve. Decorate with lychees and lime peel. Makes 6 servings.

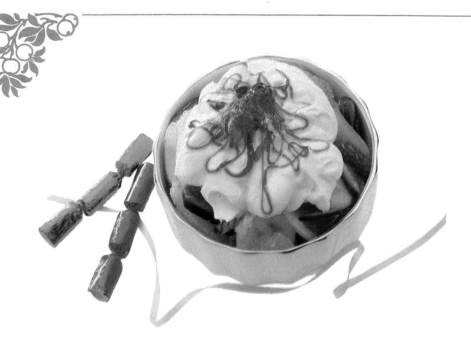

Frostie Fruit Brûlées

2 oranges
2 eating apples
2 figs
2 bananas
1 cup seedless grapes, halved
2 tablespoons Marsala wine
2-1/2 cups whipping cream
3/4 cup superfine sugar
1/4 cup boiling water

Using a sharp knife, cut orange peel away from flesh including white pith. Cut in between membrane to remove segments; place in a bowl. Cut apples into quarters; remove cores and slice thinly. Cut figs in thin wedges and slice bananas.

Gently combine all fruit and wine in bowl. Divide fruit among 6 individual dishes. In a bowl, whip cream until very thick. Spoon whipped cream evenly over fruit. Chill until ready to serve.

In a saucepan, heat sugar and water, stirring occasionally, until sugar has dissolved. Boil rapidly until syrup turns a golden brown color. Allow bubbles to subside, then drizzle caramel over top of fruit brûlées. Serve immediately. Makes 6 servings.

Festive Cheesecake

1-1/2 (8-oz.) pkgs. cream cheese
2/3 cup fromage frais
2 eggs, separated
1 tablespoon plus 1 teaspoon Grenadine syrup
1/3 cup Marsala wine
1 tablespoon plus 2 teaspoons plain gelatin
3 tablespoons water
1 starfruit, sliced
2 figs, sliced
10 kumquats, sliced
Melon balls
Seedless green and black grapes, halved
Holly sprigs and additional kumquat slices to
    decorate

Crust:
1/4 cup butter
1 tablespoon light corn syrup
2 cups vanilla wafer crumbs

To prepare crust, gently heat butter and syrup in a saucepan until melted. Stir in vanilla wafer crumbs and press into bottom of a 9-inch spring-form pan. To prepare filling, beat cream cheese, fromage frais, egg yolks, 1 tablespoon Grenadine syrup and 2 tablespoons wine in a bowl until smooth. In a small bowl, sprinkle gelatin over water and let stand until softened. Stand bowl in saucepan of hot water and stir until dissolved and quite hot. Stir gelatin into cheesecake mixture and let stand until thickened. In a bowl, whisk egg whites until stiff. Fold egg whites into cheesecake mixture until well blended and smooth. Pour over crust. Shake to level top and chill until set.

In a bowl, place all fruits. In a saucepan, heat remaining Grenadine syrup and wine until hot but not boiling. Pour over fruit and let stand until cold. Drain liquid into saucepan. Arrange fruit over top of cheesecake. Boil liquid until syrupy, brush fruit to glaze. Cut in slices to serve. Decorate with holly sprigs and additional kumquat slices. Makes 8 servings.

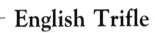

Chocolate Cherry Slice

Cake:
6 (1-oz.) squares semi-sweet chocolate
4 eggs
1/4 cup superfine sugar
1/3 cup all-purpose flour

Filling:
1 cup unsweetened marron purée
4 (1-oz.) squares semi-sweet chocolate, melted
1-1/4 cups whipping cream
3 tablespoons cherry jam
1 cup sweet cherries, pitted, halved

Preheat oven to 350F (175C). Line a 13" x 9" jelly roll pan with waxed paper. To prepare cake, break up chocolate; place in a bowl over a saucepan of hand-hot water. Stir occasionally until melted and smooth.

In a bowl, whisk eggs and sugar until thick and pale and a trail is left when whisk is lifted. Stir in chocolate until evenly blended. Sift in flour and fold in gently until evenly mixed. Pour mixture into prepared pan and shake to level. Bake in oven 20 to 25 minutes or until firm to touch. Remove from oven. Cover with a damp tea towel and let stand until cold. To prepare filling, process marron in a food processor fitted with a metal blade to a purée. Add chocolate and process until smooth. In a small bowl, whip cream until thick. Place 1/3 of whipped cream into a pastry bag fitted with small star nozzle. Fold remaining whipped cream into chocolate mixture.

Remove cake from pan. Remove paper, trim edges and cut into 3 short strips across width. Spread 2 strips of cake with jam. Cover each with 1/3 of filling. Spread smoothly. Arrange 1/3 of cherry halves on each and stack layers on a serving plate. Top with remaining cake layer. Spread top and sides of cake evenly with remaining filling and pipe scrolls of whipping cream around top edge. Decorate with remaining cherry halves. Chill until needed. Makes 10 servings.

English Trifle

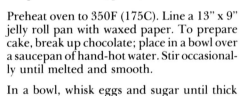

2 eggs
2 egg yolks
1 tablespoon plus 2 teaspoons superfine sugar
1-1/4 cups milk
1 teaspoon vanilla extract
2 tablespoons Madeira wine
1 tablespoon brandy
20 sponge fingers
2 tablespoons raspberry jam
1-1/2 cups raspberries, thawed if frozen
1-1/4 cups whipping cream
Angelica leaves to decorate
Vanilla cookies, if desired

To prepare custard, whisk whole eggs, egg yolks and sugar in a bowl until well blended. In a saucepan, bring milk and vanilla to boil. Pour over eggs in bowl, stirring thoroughly. Rinse out saucepan and strain custard through a sieve back into saucepan. Stirring continuously, cook over a gentle heat until thick but do not boil. Let stand until cold. In a small bowl, mix wine and brandy. Dip 1 sponge finger at a time into wine mixture. Spread with some jam and sandwich together with another dipped sponge finger. Place in bottom of a glass dish.

Repeat with remaining sponge fingers to cover bottom of dish. Pour remaining wine mixture over sponge fingers and cover with 2/3 of raspberries. In a bowl, whip cream until soft peaks form. Fold 2/3 of whipped cream into cold custard until well blended and smooth. Pour custard over raspberries in bowl. Place remaining whipped cream in a pastry bag fitted with a star nozzle. Pipe a border and decorate with angelica leaves and remaining raspberries. Serve with cookies, if desired. Chill until needed. Makes 8 servings.

White & Dark Chocolate Pots

4 (1-oz.) squares white chocolate
4 (1-oz.) squares semi-sweet chocolate
4 eggs, separated
1 tablespoon rum
1 tablespoon Cointreau liqueur
Orange peel spirals to decorate

Break up each chocolate and place in a separate bowl. Set each over a saucepan of hand-hot water. Stir occasionally until melted and smooth. Stir 2 egg yolks into each. Stir rum into semi-sweet chocolate and Cointreau into white chocolate until evenly blended.

In a bowl, stiffly beat egg whites. Add 1/2 to each chocolate mixture. Fold in carefully until each mixture is evenly blended and smooth.

Spoon alternate spoonfuls of each mixture evenly into 8 small dessert dishes. Leave in a cool place to set. Decorate with orange peel spirals. Makes 8 servings.

Festive Meringues

1-1/2 cups mixed glacé fruits, chopped
2 tablespoons plus 2 teaspoons Strega liqueur
1 cup whipping cream
1/4 cup plain yogurt
1 starfruit, thinly sliced, to decorate

Meringue:
2 egg whites
1/2 cup superfine sugar

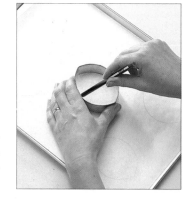

Preheat oven to 250F (120C). Line 2 baking sheets with waxed paper. Draw 5 oval shapes on each using a 2-1/2-inch oval cutter. Invert paper.

In a bowl, whisk egg whites until stiff. Whisk in sugar a little at a time, whisking thoroughly until thick and soft peaks form. Place mixture in a large pastry bag fitted with a medium star nozzle. Pipe shells of meringue around each oval shape, then fill in centers, making sure there are no gaps. Bake in oven 1-1/2 to 2 hours or until meringues are dry, crisp and lift off paper. Cool and store in an airtight container until needed. In a bowl, mix glacé fruit and liqueur and cover.

In a bowl, whip cream and yogurt until thick. Add 2/3 of glacé fruit and all liqueur. Fold in until just mixed. Spoon mixture onto each meringue. Decorate with starfruit slices and remaining glacé fruit. Makes 10 servings.

Saucy Chocolate Pudding

3 (1-oz.) squares white chocolate
3 (1-oz.) squares milk chocolate
3 (1-oz.) squares semi-sweet chocolate
3 egg yolks
2 teaspoons finely grated grapefruit peel
2 teaspoons grapefruit juice
1 tablespoon ginger wine
1 tablespoon Southern Comfort liqueur
3/4 cup softened butter
2/3 cup whipping cream
3 tablespoons fromage frais
Grapefuit slices and mint sprigs to decorate

Grapefruit Sauce:
Finely grated peel and juice 1 grapefruit
Water
2 teaspoons cornstarch
1 tablespoon superfine sugar

Break up each chocolate and place in separate bowls. Set each over a saucepan of hand-hot water. Stir occasionally until melted and smooth. Stir an egg yolk into each. Stir grapefruit peel and juice into white chocolate, ginger wine into milk chocolate and Southern Comfort into semi-sweet chocolate until smooth. Let stand until cold. Beat butter until light and fluffy. Whip cream until thick. Add 1/3 of each to chocolate mixtures and fold in until smooth and evenly blended. Line 6 individual molds with plastic wrap. Divide milk chocolate mixture between molds, making 1 layer.

Repeat with white chocolate layer and finally semi-sweet chocolate layer. Tap molds to level and freeze until firm or until needed. To prepare sauce, measure grapefruit juice and peel and enough water to measure 3/4 cup. Blend juice, cornstarch and sugar. Bring to a boil, stirring constantly. Cook gently 30 seconds; cool. Invert molds 20 minutes before serving. Pour grapefruit sauce around bottom. Decorate with grapefruit and mint. Makes 6 servings.

Kumquat & Cranberry Tarts

3/4 cup superfine sugar
1 cup water
8 oz. kumquats, sliced
1-1/2 cups cranberries
2 (3-oz.) pkgs. cream cheese, softened
1/3 cup plain yogurt
1 teaspoon arrowroot

Walnut Pastry:
1-1/2 cups all-purpose flour
1/2 cup butter
1/2 cup chopped walnuts
1/4 cup superfine sugar
1 egg, beaten

To prepare pastry, sift flour into a bowl. Cut butter into flour finely until mixture resembles fine bread crumbs. Stir in walnuts, sugar and egg. With a fork, mix to form a soft dough.

Knead on a lightly floured surface. Roll out and line 6 (4-1/2-inch) fluted flan pans. Trim edges, prick bottom and chill 30 minutes. Preheat oven to 375F (190C). Gently heat sugar and water in a saucepan until dissolved. Bring to a boil. Add kumquats and cook 3 minutes or until tender. Strain into a sieve. Return 1/3 of syrup to pan; reserve remaining syrup. Add cranberries to syrup in saucepan. Bring to a boil, cover and cook 3 minutes or until tender. Strain into a sieve. Keep syrups and fruits separate. Bake pastries 10 to 15 minutes or until lightly browned. Let stand until cold.

In a bowl, beat cream cheese and yogurt. Spread over bottom of pastries. Arrange alternate circles of kumquats and cranberries on cream cheese mixture. Blend 1/2 teaspoon of arrowroot into each syrup and bring each to boil separately. Glaze kumquats with clear syrup and cranberries with red syrup. Let stand until set. Makes 8 servings.

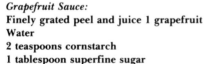
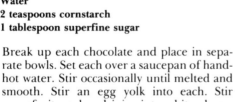
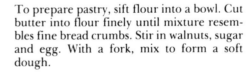
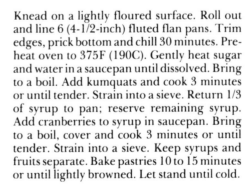

Tipsy Fruit Fool

1 lb. cooking apples, peeled, sliced
1-1/4 cups dried apricots, pre-soaked
1/4 cup superfine sugar
Peel and juice 3 satsumas
2 tablespoons apricot brandy
1/3 cup fromage frais
Chocolate curls to decorate

In a saucepan, combine apples, apricots, sugar and satsuma peel and juice. Bring to a boil. Cover and cook until apples and apricots are tender. Remove satsuma peel and reserve some for decoration. Let stand until cold.

In a food processor fitted with a metal blade, process apple mixture to a purée. Add apricot brandy and fromage frais and process until well blended. Divide mixture among individual glasses and chill until needed.

Using a sharp knife, cut reserved peel in thin strips. Decorate desserts with satsuma peel strips and chocolate curls. Makes 6 servings.

Mandarin Fig Sorbet

1/2 cup superfine sugar
2/3 cup plus 3 tablespoons water
Peel and juice 4 mandarins
6 green figs
2 teaspoons plain gelatin
2 egg whites
Mandarin shell halves, if desired
Fig slices and mint sprigs to decorate

In a saucepan, heat sugar and 2/3 cup of water, stirring occasionally, until dissolved. Add mandarin peel and figs. Bring to a boil, cover and simmer 10 minutes. Let stand until cold.

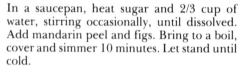

Remove mandarin peel. Pour remaining liquid and figs into a food processor fitted with a metal blade. Process to a purée. Sieve mixture into a bowl. In a small bowl, sprinkle gelatin over 3 tablespoons of water and let stand to soften 2 to 3 minutes. Stand bowl in a saucepan of hot water and stir until dissolved and quite hot. Add gelatin and mandarin juice to fig purée; stir until well blended. Pour into a plastic container. Cover and freeze 2 hours or until partially frozen but still soft.

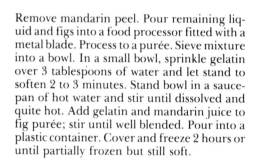

Spoon mixture into food processor and process until creamy, well blended and smooth. In a bowl, whisk egg whites until stiff. Fold in fig purée mixture until smooth. Return mixture to container. Cover and freeze until firm or until needed. Soften 15 minutes before serving in scoops. Serve in mandarin shell halves, if desired. Decorate with fresh fig slices and mint sprigs. Makes 6 servings.

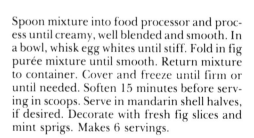

Coffee Chiffon Desserts

1/4 cup butter
3 tablespoons light corn syrup
2 cups vanilla wafer crumbs
2/3 cup whipping cream, whipped, and liqueur coffee beans to decorate

Filling:
3 tablespoons cornstarch
1/4 cup superfine sugar
1 tablespoon instant coffee granules
1-1/4 cups milk
2 eggs, separated
1 tablespoon plus 2 teaspoons plain gelatin
3 tablespoons hot water
1-1/4 cups whipping cream

In a saucepan, heat butter and corn syrup until melted. Stir in cookie crumbs and mix together evenly. Divide mixture among 8 plastic wrap-lined tiny molds and press mixture evenly over bottom and up sides of molds. Chill. To prepare filling, mix cornstarch, sugar, coffee and milk in a saucepan. Bring to a boil, stirring constantly, and cook 2 minutes. Remove from heat. Beat in egg yolks. In a small bowl, sprinkle gelatin over hot water; let stand to soften. Set bowl in a saucepan of hot water. Stir until dissolved and quite hot. Stir gelatin into coffee mixture and let stand until thick but not set.

In a small bowl, whisk egg whites until stiff. In a medium bowl, whip cream until thick. Fold egg whites and whipped cream evenly into coffee mixture. Divide mixture among molds, filling each to top. Cover and chill. To serve, invert molds onto serving plates; remove plastic wrap.

To decorate, place whipped cream in a pastry bag fitted with a star nozzle. Pipe around bottom of molds. Decorate with coffee beans. Makes 8 servings.

Amaretti Meringue Bombes

1 tablespoon butter, melted
20 Amaretti cookies (macaroons), crushed finely
12 oz. raspberries, thawed if frozen
1 tablespoon plus 1 teaspoon powdered sugar
Additional raspberries and mint sprigs to decorate
Amaretti cookies (macaroons), if desired

Filling:
2 cups coarsely crushed meringues
2-1/2 cups whipping cream
1/4 cup Amaretti cookies (macaroons), broken in small pieces
1/4 cup maraschino cherries, chopped
1/4 cup chocolate morsels

Brush insides of 8 tiny molds with melted butter. Divide crushed cookies among molds and shake well to coat evenly. Chill.

To prepare filling, mix meringues, cookie pieces, cherries and chocolate in a bowl. Stir to mix well. In another bowl, whip cream to soft peaks. Add meringue mixture to whipped cream and fold in very gently until evenly mixed. Fill each mold with meringue mixture, pressing down to pack evenly. Cover and freeze until needed. In a food processor fitted with a metal blade, process raspberries and powdered sugar to a purée. Sieve raspberry purée into a bowl.

Just before serving, dip each mold into hand-hot water and invert onto serving plates. Decorate with raspberries and mint sprigs. Serve with raspberry purée and cookies, if desired. Makes 8 servings.

Lime & Tangerine Gâteau

3 eggs, separated
2 (4-oz.) pkgs. cream cheese, softened
1/2 cup superfine sugar
Finely grated peel and juice 2 tangerines
Finely grated peel and juice 2 limes
1 tablespoon plus 2 teaspoons plain gelatin
3 tablespoons water
1 pound cake
2/3 cup whipping cream
3 tablespoons fromage frais
1/4 cup chopped pistachio nuts
Lime and tangerine wedges to decorate

To prepare filling, beat egg yolks, cream cheese and sugar in a bowl with a wooden spoon until smooth. Stir in grated fruit peel and 1/2 of juices.

In a small bowl, sprinkle gelatin over water and let stand to soften. Stand bowl in a saucepan of hot water and stir until dissolved and quite hot. Stir into cheese mixture and let stand until thick. Line a deep 7-inch-square pan with plastic wrap. Cut cake into 36 thin slices and line bottom and sides of pan with slices. Sprinkle with 1/3 of fruit juice. In a bowl, whisk egg whites until stiff; fold egg whites into cheese mixture. Pour 1/2 of cheese mixture into pan. Cover with a layer of cake and remaining cheese mixture; sprinkle with 1/3 of fruit juice.

Top with remaining cake and fruit juice. Cover with plastic wrap and chill until set; leave in pan until required. Remove gâteau from pan and remove plastic wrap carefully. In a bowl, whip cream and fromage frais until thick. Spoon 1/4 of mixture into a pastry bag fitted with a small star nozzle. Spread remaining cream evenly over gâteau and press pistachio nuts onto all sides to coat evenly. Pipe a shell border around top of gâteau and decorate with fruit wedges. Makes 12 servings.

Plum & Apple Kuchen

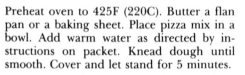

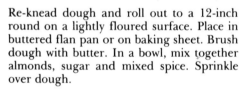

1 (6-oz.) pkg. pizza crust mix
Warm water
2 tablespoons butter, melted
3/4 cup ground almonds
1/4 cup superfine sugar
1 teaspoon ground mixed spice
1 lb. cooking apples, peeled, cored, sliced
2 lb. plums, pitted, halved
1/3 cup plum jam, boiled, sieved
1 tablespoon flaked almonds

Preheat oven to 425F (220C). Butter a flan pan or a baking sheet. Place pizza mix in a bowl. Add warm water as directed by instructions on packet. Knead dough until smooth. Cover and let stand for 5 minutes.

Re-knead dough and roll out to a 12-inch round on a lightly floured surface. Place in buttered flan pan or on baking sheet. Brush dough with butter. In a bowl, mix together almonds, sugar and mixed spice. Sprinkle over dough.

Arrange apple slices and plum halves in a circular pattern over almond mixture. Bake in oven 20 to 30 minutes or until dough is well risen and filling is tender. Cool on a wire rack. Brush with plum jam and sprinkle with flaked almonds. Makes 12 servings.

Rum Truffle Cake

7 (1-oz.) squares semi-sweet chocolate
1/2 cup unsalted butter
1/4 cup dark rum
3 eggs, separated
1/2 cup superfine sugar
3/4 cup all-purpose flour
1/2 cup ground almonds

Filling & Icing:
7 (1-oz.) squares semi-sweet chocolate
1-1/4 cups whipping cream
1 tablespoon dark rum
2 (1-oz.) squares white chocolate, grated

In a bowl, whisk egg whites until stiff. Fold 1/3 at a time into chocolate mixture until all egg whites are incorporated. Pour mixture into prepared pan. Bake in oven 45 to 55 minutes or until firm to touch in center. Turn out of pan and cool on a wire rack.

Preheat oven to 350F (175C). Butter and flour a 2-1/2-inch deep 8-inch-round cake pan. Line bottom with a circle of waxed paper.

Place chocolate and butter in a bowl over hand-hot water. Stir occasionally until melted. Add rum and stir well.

To prepare filling, melt 4 squares of chocolate with 1/4 cup of whipping cream in a bowl set over hot water. Stir in rum until well blended. Let stand until cool. To prepare icing, whip 1/2 cup of whipping cream in a bowl until thick. Add 1/2 of rum-chocolate to whipped cream and fold in until smooth.

Place egg yolks and sugar in a bowl over a saucepan of simmering water. Whisk until thick and pale. Remove bowl from saucepan. Continue to whisk until mixture leaves a trail when whisk has been lifted. Stir chocolate mixture into egg yolk mixture until evenly blended. In a small bowl, mix flour and ground almonds. Add to chocolate mixture; fold in carefully using a spatula.

Cut cake in half. Sandwich together with chocolate icing and spread remainder over top and sides. Chill cake and remaining rum-chocolate mixture in bowl. Melt remaining chocolate with whipping cream in a bowl set over hot water. Stir until smooth and cool until thick. Spread chocolate mixture over cake to cover evenly. Shape rum-chocolate mixture into 16 truffles. Coat in grated white chocolate. Arrange truffles on top of cake and chill to set. Makes 10 servings.

In another bowl, combine flour, mixed spice, ground almonds, brown sugar, butter, molasses and eggs with a wooden spoon, then beat until smooth and glossy. Add mixed fruit to cake mixture; stir until evenly mixed.

Spoon mixture into prepared pan. Level top with back of a metal spoon, making a slight depression in center. Bake in oven 3-1/4 to 3-1/2 hours. Test with a skewer; when inserted in center, skewer should come out clean. Cool in pan. Invert cake, remove paper and place on a cake plate.

Christmas Cake

Cake:
6-3/4 cups mixed dried fruit
3/4 cup quartered glacé cherries
1/2 cup cut mixed peel
3/4 cup flaked almonds
Finely grated peel and juice 1 orange
1/2 cup brandy or sherry
3 cups all-purpose flour
1 tablespoon ground mixed spice
2/3 cup ground almonds
1-1/2 cups dark-brown sugar
1-1/2 cups butter, softened
2 tablespoons molasses
5 eggs

Decoration:
3 tablespoons apricot jam, boiled, sieved
1-3/4 lb. marzipan
2-lb. ready-to-roll fondant icing (sugar paste)
Red and green food colorings
Red and green ribbon

Brush top and side of cake with apricot jam. Knead marzipan and roll out to 1/4-inch thickness. Cover top and sides of cake; trim to fit at bottom. Roll out fondant icing on a lightly sugared surface. Cover cake. Press icing over top and down side of cake. Trim off excess icing at bottom.

Preheat oven to 275F (135C). Line a 2-1/2-inch deep 8-inch-square or 2-1/2-inch deep 9-inch-round cake pan with a double thickness of greased parchment paper, extending parchment paper above sides of pan. Place pan on a double parchment paper-lined baking sheet. In a large bowl, combine dried fruit, cherries, mixed peel and flaked almonds until well mixed. Add orange peel and juice and brandy or sherry; mix well.

Knead trimmings together; color 1/3 red and remainder green with food colorings. Make tiny berries with some of the red icing. Roll and cut out holly leaves from green icing. Mark in veins with knife; let stand until set. Arrange on top of cake with berries. Cut out 'NOEL' from red icing and place on cake. Let cake stand until dry. Tie with ribbon. Makes 40 servings.

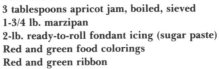

Festive Mince Pies

1-1/2 cups mincemeat
1 egg white
Red and green food colorings

Pastry:
3 cups all-purpose flour
3/4 cup butter
2 tablespoons superfine sugar
1 egg yolk
Cold water

Preheat oven to 400F (205C). To prepare pastry, sift flour into a bowl. Cut butter into flour finely until mixture resembles bread crumbs. Using a fork, stir in sugar, egg yolk and enough cold water to form a soft dough. Knead on a lightly floured surface.

Roll out pastry thinly and cut out 20 (3-inch) rounds and 20 (2-inch) rounds. Line 20 tart pans with large pastry circles. Prick bottom of each with a fork and half-fill with mincemeat. Brush edges of each pastry lid with water, invert and press on top of tart to seal edges. Pierce a hole in center to allow steam to escape. Using all pastry trimmings, roll out thinly. Using a holly leaf cutter, cut out 40 holly leaves; mark veins with a knife. Roll tiny balls of pastry to form berries. Brush top of each mince pie with egg white. Arrange holly leaves and berries on top.

Bake in oven 15 minutes until cooked but not pale. Divide egg white between 2 cups; color 1 red and 1 green with food colorings. Brush leaves green and berries red. Bake in oven another 5 minutes. Cool on a wire rack. Makes 20 pies.

Southern Comfort Cake

1-1/4 cups butter
1/2 cup plus 2 tablespoons light corn syrup
1-1/4 cups Southern Comfort, sherry or cider
Finely grated peel and juice 1 orange
Finely grated peel and juice 1 lemon
6-1/4 cups mixed dried fruit
2-1/2 cups chopped dried apricots
2-1/4 cups chopped dried dates
3/4 teaspoon baking soda
3 eggs
3-1/2 cups whole-wheat self-rising flour
2 teaspoons ground allspice
1/2 cup apricot jam, boiled, sieved
2-1/4 cups assorted nuts such as pecans, brazil
    nuts, hazelnuts, pine nuts
Whole dried apricot and dates
Holly sprigs to decorate
Ribbon

Grease and double-line a 10" x 8" x 2" baking pan with waxed paper. Place pan on a double-waxed-paper-lined baking sheet. In a large saucepan, combine butter, corn syrup, Southern Comfort, sherry or cider and orange and lemon peel and juice. Heat until almost boiling. Stir in mixed fruit, apricots and dates, stirring until well blended. Let stand until almost cold. Preheat oven to 300F (150C). Add soda, eggs, flour and allspice and stir until mixture is thoroughly mixed.

Spoon mixture into prepared pan. Level top and bake in oven 2-1/4 to 2-1/2 hours or until cake feels firm in center. Test with a skewer; when inserted in center, skewer should come out clean. Cool in pan, invert and wrap in foil until needed. Cut cake in 6 pieces. Brush each piece with apricot jam. Arrange nuts and fruit over top and glaze with remaining jam. Let stand until set. Decorate with holly sprigs tied with ribbon. Makes 6 individual cakes.

Mini Christmas Cakes

1 (8-inch) square Christmas Cake, page 54
  or Glacé Fruit Cake, page 57
4 (4-inch) square cake cards
1/3 cup apricot jam, boiled, sieved
2 lb. white marzipan
Red, green and silver food colorings
Cornstarch
1 egg white
2-1/4 yards each red, green, silver ribbon
1-1/2 lb. ready-to-roll fondant icing (sugar
  paste)
Powdered sugar
Red, green and silver dragees
Red and green cake candle

Sprinkle surface of fondant icing with powdered sugar. Cut icing in half; place half in a
plastic bag and seal. Knead remaining icing
until smooth; roll out to an 8-inch square.
Place icing over 1 cake with marzipan. With
hands covered with cornstarch, smooth top
and sides and trim off excess icing around
bottom of cake. Repeat to cover second cake.
Knead icing trimmings together.

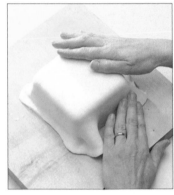

Cut cake in 4 small square cakes; place each
on a cake board. Brush evenly with apricot
jam. Cut marzipan in 4 pieces. Color 1 piece
pale pink and 1 pale green with food colorings. Roll out 1 piece at a time to about 6
inches square on a lightly sugared surface.
Place over cake and trim to fit; reserve marzipan trimmings. Let white marzipan cakes dry
in a warm place. Using a crimper dipped in
cornstarch, crimp top and bottom edge of
pink and green cakes.

Press silver and red dragees around top edge
and bottom of cake; secure with egg white, if
necessary. Repeat with green and silver
dragees on remaining cake. Tie silver and
green and silver and red ribbon around each
respective cake; tie with pretty bows.

Color remaining green and pink marzipan
bright green and red by adding a few more
drops of food colorings. Roll out green thinly
and cut out about 20 holly leaves using a holly
leaf cutter. Shape red marzipan in tiny holly
berries. Arrange holly leaves and berries over
top of cake, securing each with some egg
white. Using green and red ribbon, measure
and cut ribbon to fit round outside of each
cake.

Roll out icing trimmings on a surface dusted
lightly with cornstarch. Using a tiny star-
shaped cutter, cut out 26 stars. Using food
coloring, paint surfaces of 14 stars silver, 6
stars red and 6 stars green. Let stand until
dry. Arrange green and silver stars on green
and silver cake and red and silver stars on red
and silver cake. Place a candle in center of
each. Let stand until dry. Makes 4 individual
cakes.

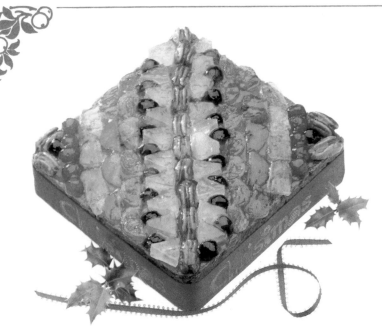

Glacé Fruit Cake

Cake:
2-1/2 cups mixed glacé fruit, chopped
3/4 cup dried apricots, chopped
1 cup chopped pecans
Finely grated peel and juice 1 lemon
3 cups all-purpose flour
1 teaspoon baking powder
1-1/2 teaspoons ground mixed spice
1-2/3 cups ground almonds
1-3/4 cups superfine sugar
1-1/2 cups butter, softened
4 eggs

Topping:
1/4 cup apricot jam
2 teaspoons water
Mixed glacé fruit and nuts
Ribbon and holly sprigs to decorate

Preheat oven to 275F (135C). Line a 2-1/2-inch deep 8-inch-square cake pan or a 2-1/2-inch deep 9-inch-round pan with a double thickness of greased waxed paper, extending greased waxed paper above edge of pan. Place pan on baking sheet lined with a double thickness of waxed paper.

Combine glacé fruit, apricots, nuts and lemon peel and juice. Sift flour, baking powder and mixed spice into a bowl. Mix in ground almonds, sugar, butter and eggs, then beat 2 to 3 minutes or until smooth and glossy. Stir in mixed fruit and nuts.

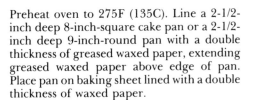

Spoon mixture into prepared pan. Smooth top and bake 2-1/4 to 2-1/2 hours or until cake feels firm and springy. Cool in pan, then turn out and wrap in foil. In a saucepan, bring jam and water to a boil, stirring constantly, then sieve. Brush top of cake with jam. Arrange fruit and nuts over top and brush with remaining jam. Let stand until set. Decorate with ribbon and holly. Makes 30 servings.

Tiny Chocolate Logs

3 eggs
2 tablespoons plus 2 teaspoons superfine sugar
1/4 cup all-purpose flour
1 tablespoon cocoa powder
Powdered sugar, if desired
Marzipan toadstools and holly sprigs to decorate

Filling:
1-1/4 cups whipping cream
4 (1-oz.) squares semisweet chocolate

Preheat oven to 400F (205C). Line a 1-inch deep 12-inch baking sheet with waxed paper. Place eggs and sugar in a bowl set over a saucepan of simmering water. Whisk until thick and pale.

Remove bowl from saucepan; continue whisking until mixture leaves a trail when whisk is lifted. Sift flour and cocoa onto surface of mixture; fold in carefully until mixture is evenly blended. Pour mixture onto prepared baking sheet; spread carefully to edges. Bake in oven 8 to 10 minutes or until firm to touch. Cool a few minutes and remove cake. Remove waxed paper, trim edges and cut cake in half. To prepare filling, place 1/4 cup whipping cream and chocolate broken into pieces in a bowl set over saucepan of hot water. Stir occasionally until melted. Whip remaining cream until almost thick.

When chocolate has cooled, fold it carefully into whipped cream. Using 1/3 of chocolate cream, spread evenly over each cake. Roll each in a firm roll from long edge. Wrap in plastic wrap and chill 20 minutes or until firm. Cut each roll in 6 lengths. Spread each with remaining chocolate cream using a small palette knife; mark cream in lines. Sprinkle with powdered sugar, if desired. Decorate with toadstools and holly. Refrigerate until ready to serve. Makes 12 servings.

Christmas Gift Cakes

1-1/4 cups self-rising flour
1 teaspoon baking powder
1/3 cup hazelnuts, toasted, ground
3/4 cup superfine sugar
3/4 cup butter, softened
3 eggs
2 tablespoons apricot jam, boiled, sieved
1-1/4 lb. ready-to-roll fondant icing (sugar paste)
Red and green food colorings
Powdered sugar

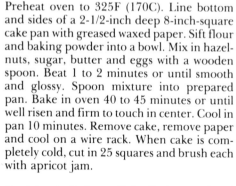

Preheat oven to 325F (170C). Line bottom and sides of a 2-1/2-inch deep 8-inch-square cake pan with greased waxed paper. Sift flour and baking powder into a bowl. Mix in hazelnuts, sugar, butter and eggs with a wooden spoon. Beat 1 to 2 minutes or until smooth and glossy. Spoon mixture into prepared pan. Bake in oven 40 to 45 minutes or until well risen and firm to touch in center. Cool in pan 10 minutes. Remove cake, remove paper and cool on a wire rack. When cake is completely cold, cut in 25 squares and brush each with apricot jam.

Cut icing in 3 pieces. Color 2 pieces red and green with food colorings. Cut a small piece off each piece of icing and reserve for trimming. Roll out white icing thinly on a lightly sugared surface. Cut in 8 (2-inch) squares.

Cover 8 cakes with squares of white icing, tucking excess icing under base of each cake. Repeat with remaining icing and cakes, covering 8 in red and 9 in green. Using reserved icing, roll out thin lengths and trim each cake with "ribbons and bows." Let dry in a warm place. Makes 25 cakes.

Maraschino Fruit Ring

1 cup self-rising flour
3/4 cup light-brown sugar
1/2 cup butter, softened
3 eggs
1/2 cup pecans, chopped
1/2 cup dark raisins
1/2 cup red maraschino cherries, drained, sliced
1/2 cup green glacé cherries, drained, sliced
1/2 cup powdered sugar, sifted
2 tablespoons plus 2 teaspoons maraschino cherry syrup
6 red and 6 green maraschino cherries, sliced
Holly sprig to decorate

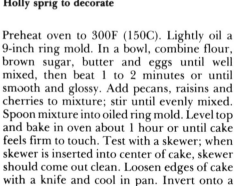

Preheat oven to 300F (150C). Lightly oil a 9-inch ring mold. In a bowl, combine flour, brown sugar, butter and eggs until well mixed, then beat 1 to 2 minutes or until smooth and glossy. Add pecans, raisins and cherries to mixture; stir until evenly mixed. Spoon mixture into oiled ring mold. Level top and bake in oven about 1 hour or until cake feels firm to touch. Test with a skewer; when skewer is inserted into center of cake, skewer should come out clean. Loosen edges of cake with a knife and cool in pan. Invert onto a wire rack.

In a bowl, combine powdered sugar and enough cherry syrup to make a consistency of thick cream. Spoon icing over cold cake. Arrange cherry slices in clusters around top of cake. Let stand until set. Decorate with holly sprig. Makes 10 servings.

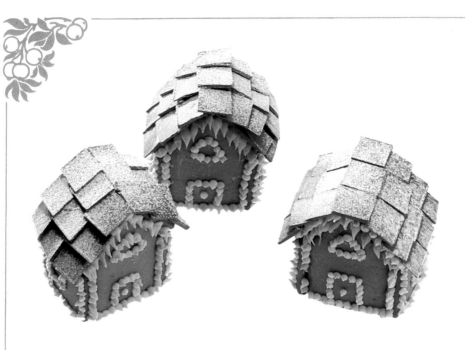

Gingerbread Houses

2 tablespoons light corn syrup
2 tablespoons molasses
2 tablespoons light-brown sugar
1/4 cup butter
1-1/2 cups all-purpose flour
1-1/2 teaspoons ground ginger
1/2 teaspoon baking soda
1 egg, beaten
4 (1-oz.) squares white chocolate
4 (1-oz.) squares semi-sweet chocolate
Pink, green and yellow food colorings
Powdered sugar

Preheat oven to 400F (205C). Line 2 baking sheets with waxed paper. In a saucepan, combine corn syrup, molasses, brown sugar and butter. Heat gently, stirring occasionally, until melted.

Sift flour and ginger into a bowl. Stir baking soda into melted mixture; add to flour with enough beaten egg to mix to form a soft dough. Knead on a lightly floured surface until smooth and free from cracks. Cut off 1/3 of dough and wrap in plastic wrap.

Roll out remaining 2/3 of dough thinly and cut out 32 (1-1/2-inch) squares of dough. Place spaced apart on a prepared baking sheet. Roll out remaining dough and cut out 16 (2-1/2- x 1-1/2-inches) rectangles. Measure and mark 1 inch down side of each rectangle. Cut from each mark to center of oblong to shape a "pitch" for "roof." Place on prepared baking sheet and bake in oven 8 to 10 minutes or until golden brown. Cool on a wire rack.

Break up and place white and dark chocolate into separate bowls over hand-hot water. Stir occasionally until melted. Divide white chocolate among 3 small bowls; color pink and green and yellow with food colorings. Assemble each house using semi-sweet chocolate to stick 2 side and 2 end walls together and 2 roof pieces in position. Let stand until set. Spread remaining chocolate over waxed paper.

When chocolate is almost set, invert onto piece of waxed paper. Peel off waxed paper and cut in 3/4-inch squares for roof tiles. Secure tiles onto roof with melted chocolate, starting at bottom of each roof and working to top. Fill 3 pastry bags with colored chocolate. Snip off points and pipe in doors, windows and colored beads of chocolate down all seams. Let stand until set. Dust with powdered sugar. Makes 8 houses.

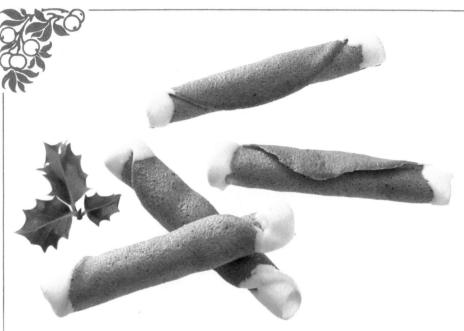

Chocolate Cigarettes

2 egg whites
1/3 cup plus 1 tablespoon superfine sugar
1/4 cup plus 3 tablespoons all-purpose flour
2 teaspoons cocoa powder
1/4 cup unsalted butter, melted
2 (1-oz.) squares white chocolate, melted
Holly sprigs to decorate

Preheat oven to 400F (205C). Line 2 baking sheets with waxed paper. In a bowl, whisk egg whites until stiff. Add sugar gradually, whisking well after each addition. Sift flour and cocoa over surface of mixture. Add butter and fold in carefully until mixture is evenly blended.

Place 2 spoonfuls of mixture onto each prepared baking sheet, spacing well apart. Spread each in a thin round. Bake 1 sheet at a time in oven 3 to 4 minutes. Loosen each round with a palette knife, then return to oven 1 minute.

Remove 1 chocolate round at a time and quickly roll around a greased pencil or wooden spoon handle to form a tube. Slip off and cool cigarette on a wire rack. Repeat with remaining rounds. Cook second tray of rounds, then repeat to make cigarettes. Dip both ends of each cigarette into melted chocolate. Let set on waxed paper-lined baking sheet. Store in an airtight container until needed. Decorate with holly sprigs. Makes 25 pieces.

Christmas Treats

2 eggs
1/4 cup superfine sugar
1/2 cup all-purpose flour
Additional superfine sugar
1/2 cup apricot jam, boiled, and sieved
1 lb. white marzipan
Red, green and gold food colorings

Preheat oven to 375F (190C). Line bottom and sides of a 13" x 9" jelly roll pan with greased waxed paper. Place eggs and 1/4 cup sugar in a heatproof bowl over a saucepan of simmering water. Whisk mixture until thick and pale. Remove bowl from pan. Whisk until thick, cool and mixture leaves a trail when whisk is lifted.

Sift flour onto egg mixture. Fold in carefully using a spatula until all flour has been incorporated. Pour mixture into prepared pan. Bake in oven 10 to 15 minutes or until well risen and firm to touch. Sprinkle a piece of waxed paper with additional sugar. Invert cake, peel off paper and trim off edge with a large knife. Cut cake in half down length. Spread jam to within 1/2 inch of edges. Roll up each cake in 2 long thin rolls from long edges with help of paper. Cool on a wire rack, then cut in 12 mini-rolls. Brush mini-rolls with apricot jam.

Reserve 2 oz. of marzipan. Cut remainder in half. Color 1 piece red and 1 piece green with red and green food colorings. Roll out green marzipan thinly and cut out 6 (4-1/2" x 4") rectangles. Roll up 6 mini-rolls in marzipan with seam underneath. Squeeze ends together and flute. Repeat with red marzipan. Use trimmings to cut out holly leaves and berries from green and red marzipan. Roll out remaining marzipan and trim each with lattice strips. Brush with gold food coloring and decorate with holly and berries. Makes 12 pieces.

Scottish Black Buns

2 (6-oz.) pkgs. pizza crust mix
Warm water
1 egg yolk
1 teaspoon water
Purple and green food colorings

Filling:
1 cup mixed dried fruit
1/4 cup chopped glace cherries
1/4 cup chopped flaked almonds
Finely grated peel and juice 1 orange
2 tablespoons light-brown sugar
1/4 cup butter, melted
1/2 cup all-purpose flour
1 teaspoon ground allspice
1 egg, beaten

In a bowl, combine bread mix and warm water as directed on package. Knead 5 minutes. Place in a plastic bag and let stand until filling has been made. Preheat oven to 350F (175C). Lightly flour 2 baking sheets.

In a large bowl, combine dried fruit, cherries, almonds and orange peel and juice with a wooden spoon. Add brown sugar, butter, flour, allspice and egg; stir well until all ingredients are evenly mixed.

Knead dough on a lightly floured surface and cut in 11 pieces. Roll 1 piece at a time out thinly to a 5-inch round. Brush edge of round with water; place 1 heaping spoonful of filling in center of dough.

Draw up edge of dough to cover filling. Seal in center and shape in a smooth ball. Turn bun over with seam underneath. Place on prepared baking sheet. Repeat to make 9 more buns. Prick buns all over with a fine skewer.

Roll out remaining dough very thinly. Cut out 10 thistle shapes, stems and leaves. Brush each bun with 1 teaspoon of egg yolk mixed with water to glaze. Bake in oven 25 minutes and remove from oven.

Divide remaining egg yolk in half. Color 1 half purple and one half green with food colorings. Brush thistles purple and leaves and stems green 5 minutes before end of baking time to color evenly. Return to oven 5 minutes until glaze has set and buns are golden brown. Cool on a wire rack. Makes 10 buns.

Brandy Rope Rings

1 cup butter, softened
¾ cup sugar
2½ cups all-purpose flour, sifted
1 teaspoon powdered cinnamon
3 tablespoons brandy

Preheat oven to 350F (175C). Cream butter and sugar together until light and fluffy. Stir flour and cinnamon into creamed mixture. Stir in brandy and mix well.

Turn dough onto a floured board and roll to ¼-inch thickness. Cut dough into ¾ x 5-inch strips. Twist two of the strips together to form a 'rope'.

Join the two ends of the 'ropes' together to form a circle. Repeat with remaining strips. Place circles on cookie sheets lined with baking parchment. Bake 15 minutes, or until golden brown. These cookies can be left plain, drizzled with glaze, or threaded together with ribbon. They can also be hung on the Christmas tree or boxed as gifts.

Makes about 24.

Christmas Garland

½ cup butter
1½ cups sifted, all-purpose flour
2 tablespoons superfine sugar
¼ cup lemon juice
1 egg yolk
2 to 4 tablespoons water
½ cup blanched almonds
⅓ cup candied lemon peel
¼ cup sugar
1 egg white
Few drops of almond extract
1 teaspoon grated lemon peel
20 red and green glacé cherries, chopped
Extra egg white for glazing
½ cup powdered sugar, sifted
2 teaspoons lemon juice, warmed
Nuts, glacé cherries and candied peel, for decoration

Cut butter into flour and sugar until mixture resembles coarse meal. Mix in lemon juice, egg yolk and enough water to form a firm dough. Wrap; refrigerate 8 hours. Roll to a large rectangle.

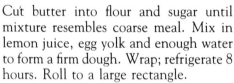

In a food processor or blender, combine next 6 ingredients. Cover; refrigerate 8 hours. Roll into a long sausage, place down the center of dough. Sprinkle filling with cherries. Brush edges of dough with water, fold over filling to form a roll. Press together firmly.

Shape roll into a circle, pressing the open ends together carefully. Place seam-side down on greased cookie sheet. Brush with egg white. Refrigerate 30 minutes. Preheat oven to 400F (205C). Bake 20 to 25 minutes, or until golden brown. Cool on a wire rack. In a small bowl, mix powdered sugar and lemon juice until smooth. Drizzle over garland. Decorate.

Makes 1 garland.

— COOKIES, CANDIES, & GIFTS —

Advent Cookies

1-1/4 cups all-purpose flour
1/3 cup butter
1/4 cup ground almonds
2 tablespoons plus 2 teaspoons superfine sugar
1 egg yolk
Cold water
1 egg white
1-1/2 cups powdered sugar, sifted
Red, green, yellow, and black food coloring
    pens
Assorted colors fine ribbon

Preheat oven to 350F (175C). Lightly flour 2 baking sheets. Sift flour into a bowl. Cut butter into flour finely until mixture resembles bread crumbs. Stir in ground almonds, sugar, egg yolk and enough cold water to form a soft dough.

Knead dough on a lightly floured surface. Roll out thinly and cut out 24 squares, rounds or ovals using a 2-1/4-inch cutter. Arrange on prepared baking sheet. Make a hole in top of each cookie with a drinking straw. Bake in oven 10 to 15 minutes or until lightly browned at edges. Cool on a wire rack.

In a bowl, combine egg white and enough powdered sugar to make a consistency of thick cream. Beat until smooth and glossy. Dip surface of each cookie into icing to cover evenly; allow excess to fall into bowl. Place on a rack to dry. When icing is dry and hard, use food coloring pens to number cookies 1 to 24 and draw a different design or message onto each cookie. Thread ribbons through holes at top and hang 1 up each day from December 1st to 24th. Makes 24 cookies.

Note:
Use remaining dough to make 1 special cookie for Christmas Day, if desired.

Brandy Snaps

1/2 cup butter
3/4 cup packed brown sugar
1/3 cup light corn syrup
4 teaspoons lemon juice
4 teaspoons brandy
1 cup all-purpose flour
1 teaspoon ground ginger

Put butter, sugar, corn syrup, lemon juice and brandy in a medium-size saucepan; stir over medium heat until butter melts and sugar dissolves. Remove from heat; sift flour and ginger into saucepan. Mix well. Allow mixture to cool completely.

Preheat oven to 375F (190C). Grease several baking sheets; line with parchment or waxed paper. For ease of handling, bake only 6 Brandy Snaps at a time, placing baking sheets in oven at 5 minute intervals. Parchment paper may be reused; wipe with a paper towel before spooning on more mixture. Drop small teaspoonfuls of mixture onto prepared baking sheets, spacing well apart. Bake 8 to 10 minutes or until very lightly browned. Have 6 wooden spoon handles or chopsticks ready to use for shaping cookies.

Allow Brandy Snaps to cool on the baking sheet for a few seconds. Remove with a spatula and wrap around handles of wooden spoons or chopsticks. When cookies are set, slide off of spoon handle or chopstick and place on a plate. If Brandy Snaps become too stiff to roll up, simply reheat for a few seconds to soften.

Makes about 36 Brandy Snaps.

Florentines

1/4 cup unsalted butter
1/3 cup whipping cream
1/2 cup packed brown sugar
Finely grated peel of 1 large lemon
2 teaspoons lemon juice
1/4 cup all-purpose flour, sifted
1/2 cup (3 oz.) blanched almonds, slivered
1/2 cup chopped mixed citrus peel
1/3 cup candied cherries, chopped
1 oz. angelica, chopped
2 tablespoons golden raisins
1 oz. dried apricots, chopped
6 oz. semisweet chocolate, chopped

Preheat oven to 350F (175C). Grease several large baking sheets; line with parchment or waxed paper. Put butter, whipping cream, sugar, lemon peel and lemon juice in a large saucepan; stir over medium heat until butter melts. Remove from heat; stir in flour, almonds and fruit. Drop teaspoonfuls of mixture onto prepared baking sheets, spacing well apart. Using a fork dipped in cold water, flatten each teaspoonful into a circle about 2-1/2 inches in diameter.

Bake 10 to 12 minutes or until lightly browned around edges. Cool on baking sheets for a few minutes then remove with a spatula to wire racks; cool completely. Melt chocolate in a small bowl placed over a pan of hot, but not boiling, water. Taking one Florentine at a time, spread flat side with chocolate. Using a fork, mark chocolate with wavy lines. Place on a plate, chocolate-side-up, and leave to set.

Makes about 28 Florentines.

Creme de Menthe Cookies

8 (1-oz.) squares semi-sweet chocolate
2 tablespoons butter
2 cups graham cracker crumbs
3/4 cup plain cake crumbs
Superfine sugar
Mint sprigs to decorate

Filling:
1/4 cup unsalted butter
3/4 cup powdered sugar, sieved
2 teaspoons Creme de Menthe

To prepare filling, beat butter in a bowl with a wooden spoon or electric mixer until soft and smooth. Gradually beat in powdered sugar and Creme de Menthe until light and fluffy.

Break up chocolate and place in a bowl with butter over a saucepan of hand-hot water. Stir occasionally until melted. Add graham cracker and cake crumbs; stir until evenly mixed and mixture forms a ball. Sprinkle a 10-inch square of foil with superfine sugar.

Roll out chocolate mixture on foil in an 8-inch square. Spread filling evenly over chocolate mixture to within 1/2 inch of edges. Roll up carefully from long edge in a smooth roll using foil. Wrap in foil and chill until firm. Cut in thin slices when needed. Decorate with mint sprigs. Makes 20 servings.

Cherry Praline Rings

1/2 cup (2 oz.) hazelnuts
2/3 cup sugar
1/2 cup butter, softened
1 egg
3 cups all-purpose flour
Pinch of salt
1 teaspoon baking powder
1 cup candied cherries, halved and thinly sliced

Glaze:
1 small egg, beaten
1 tablespoon milk
2 teaspoons sugar

To Finish:
Sugar for sprinkling

Lightly grease a small baking sheet. Put hazelnuts and 1/4 cup of the sugar in a small saucepan; stir over low heat until sugar caramelizes. Pour onto baking sheet; cool. Break into rough pieces and grind finely in a food processor or blender. Preheat oven to 350F (175C). Grease several baking sheets with butter. In a large bowl, cream butter with remaining sugar; beat in egg then praline. Sift flour, salt and baking powder into bowl; blend in with a spoon then mix with your hand to form a dough. Knead lightly to make a smooth dough.

Roll out dough on a floured surface to 1/8-inch thickness. Using a round 2-1/2-inch-fluted cookie cutter, cut out circles from dough; remove centers from circles with a round 1/2-inch-fluted cookie cutter. Place circles, slightly apart, on prepared baking sheets. Knead and roll out trimmings; cut out more circles. Mix all ingredients for glaze together; brush over circles. Decorate with candied cherries. Bake about 15 minutes or until lightly browned; sprinkle with sugar. Remove to wire racks; cool.

Makes 38 to 40 cookies.

Chocolate-Raisin Bars

1-3/4 cups all-purpose flour
Pinch of salt
8 teaspoons potato flour
1/4 cup vanilla sugar
3/4 cup butter
1/3 cup (2 oz.) raisins, chopped
8 oz. semisweet chocolate pieces

Preheat oven to 350F (175C). Sift all-purpose flour, salt, potato flour and vanilla sugar into a medium-size bowl. Cut in butter until mixture forms coarse crumbs; mix in raisins. Mix together to form a soft dough.

Roll out dough on a floured surface to a rectangle slightly smaller than an 11'' x 7'' baking pan. Place rolled-out dough in pan; press to fit. Smooth top; prick well. Bake about 25 minutes or until very lightly browned. Cool a few minutes. Using a sharp knife, mark through surface of mixture with lines to use as a guide for cutting. Let cool in pan.

Cut mixture in 20 squares; remove from pan. Place chocolate in a small bowl over a pan of gently simmering water; stir until melted and smooth. Line a baking sheet with foil. Dip bars in chocolate, coating evenly; lift out with a fork and tap gently on side of bowl to remove excess chocolate. Place on foil. Place baking sheet in a cool place until chocolate sets. If desired, any remaining chocolate can be piped over bars for decoration.

Makes 20 bars.

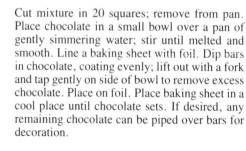

Traditional Shortbread

1/2 cup butter, softened
5 teaspoons sugar
1-1/4 cups all-purpose flour
Pinch of salt
2 tablespoons fine semolina

To Finish:
Superfine sugar for sprinkling

In a medium-size bowl, beat butter with sugar until creamy. Sift flour and salt into bowl; add semolina. Blend in with a spoon then mix with your hand to form a soft dough.

Knead dough lightly on a floured surface until smooth. Roll out to a smooth circle, about 6 inches in diameter. Very lightly flour a 7-inch shortbread mold. Place shortbread smooth-side-down in mold. Press out to fit mold exactly. Very carefully unmold shortbread onto an un-greased baking sheet. Refrigerate 1 hour. If you do not have a shortbread mold, shape dough into a neat circle; place on baking sheet. Prick well with a fork then pinch edge to decorate.

Preheat oven to 325F (165C). Bake about 35 minutes or until cooked through. Shortbread should remain pale. As soon as shortbread is removed from oven, sprinkle very lightly with superfine sugar. Cool on baking sheet about 20 minutes then very carefully remove to a wire rack to cool completely.

Makes one (7-inch) shortbread.

Christmas Shortbread

1-3/4 cups all-purpose flour
Pinch of salt
3 tablespoons cornstarch
1/4 cup sugar
1 cup butter

To Decorate:
34 blanched almonds
15 walnut halves
7 green candied cherries, cut in half
5 red candied cherries, cut in half

To Finish:
Superfine sugar for sprinkling

Sift flour, salt and cornstarch into a medium-size bowl; add sugar. Cut in butter until mixture forms coarse crumbs. Gently mix together to form a soft dough. Roll out dough on a floured surface to a circle slightly smaller than 10 inches in diameter. Place dough in a 10-inch-fluted pie pan with removable bottom. Press dough gently to fit pan exactly, pressing well into flutes. Smooth with the back of a spoon. Prick well with a fork.

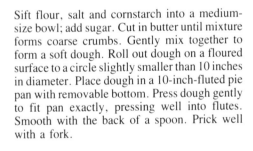

To decorate shortbread, arrange almonds in a neat ring around edge of dough. Add a ring of walnut halves, a ring of green cherries, then a ring of red cherries. Place a walnut half in the center. Refrigerate shortbread 30 minutes. Pre-heat oven to 350F (175C). Bake shortbread about 45 minutes or until lightly browned. Cool in pan. Sprinkle lightly with superfine sugar. Carefully remove from pan onto a serving plate.

Makes about 16 servings.

Almond Flowers

2-1/4 cups (8 oz.) ground almonds
1/2 cup sugar
3/4 cup powdered sugar, sifted
1 teaspoon rose water
1 teaspoon orange flower water
A few drops almond extract
3 egg yolks

Glaze:
1/4 cup sugar
1 tablespoon cool water
3 tablespoons warm water
2 egg yolks

To Decorate:
6 walnut halves, split in half
7 blanched almonds, split in half
8 pistachio nuts, split in half

In a medium-size bowl, mix ground almonds with sugars. Make a well in the center and add flavorings and egg yolks. Mix to form a stiff paste. Knead lightly until smooth. Wrap in plastic wrap. Set aside.

To make glaze, dissolve 1/4 cup sugar in cool water in a very small saucepan. Boil until caramelized. Add warm water; heat to dissolve caramelized sugar; cool. Beat in egg yolks. Preheat oven to 450F (230C). Line several baking sheets with parchment or waxed paper. Roll out almond paste to 1/4-inch thickness. Using a 2-inch flower-shaped cookie cutter, cut out flowers. Place on prepared baking sheets. Brush with glaze; decorate with nuts. Bake 5 minutes or until browned. Cool on baking sheets.

Makes about 42 flowers.

Pinwheels

3/4 cup (12 tablespoons) butter, softened
3/4 cup (12 tablespoons) sugar
1 teaspoon vanilla extract
2 eggs
4-1/2 cups all-purpose flour
2 teaspoons baking powder
2 pinches of salt
2 tablespoons unsweetened cocoa
1 teaspoon brandy
1 egg white, very lightly beaten

Divide butter and sugar equally between 2 separate bowls.

To make vanilla dough, beat 1/2 of butter and sugar until creamy; beat in vanilla and 1 egg. Sift 1/2 of flour, 1/2 of baking powder and a pinch of salt into bowl. Blend in with a spoon then mix with your hand to form a dough. Wrap in plastic wrap; chill 45 minutes. Make chocolate dough in same way, using remaining butter, sugar, egg, flour, baking powder and salt, sifting cocoa in with remaining flour and baking powder. Add brandy to chocolate dough. Wrap and chill 45 minutes.

Roll out doughs separately on a floured surface to 13'' x 11'' rectangles. Brush vanilla dough with beaten egg white; place chocolate dough on top. Trim edges to make straight. Brush chocolate dough with egg white. Roll up, starting from one long side, to form a tight roll. Wrap in plastic wrap; chill 1 hour. Preheat oven to 350F (175C). Grease several baking sheets with butter. Cut roll in 1/4-inch-thick slices; place on prepared baking sheets. Bake 20 minutes or until lightly browned. Remove to wire racks; cool.

Makes about 48 Pinwheels.

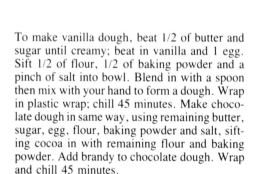

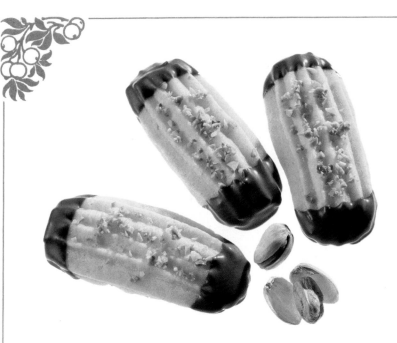

Viennese Fingers

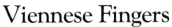

1 cup butter, softened
1/3 cup powdered sugar, sifted
1 teaspoon vanilla extract
2 cups all-purpose flour
Pinch of salt
1 tablespoon pistachio nuts, chopped

To Finish:
2 oz. semisweet chocolate pieces

Preheat oven to 350F (175C). Grease several baking sheets with butter; dust lightly with flour.

In a medium-size bowl, beat butter with powdered sugar until very light and creamy. Beat in vanilla. Sift flour and salt into bowl; mix into butter with a wooden spoon to form a soft dough. Put dough in a piping bag fitted with a 1/2-inch (10-point-star) tip. Pipe 2-1/2-inch lengths of mixture onto prepared baking sheets, spacing apart. Cut dough off at tip with a small knife when required length is reached. Sprinkle with pistachio nuts.

Bake about 20 minutes or until very lightly browned. Cool on baking sheets a few minutes then remove to wire racks to cool completely. Put chocolate in a small bowl and place over a pan of simmering water; stir until melted and smooth. Dip both ends of fingers in melted chocolate, scraping off excess on side of bowl; place on foil. Leave in a cool place until chocolate sets.

Makes about 24 cookies.

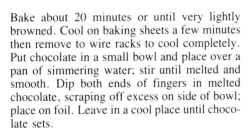

Shell Cookies

1 cup butter, softened
1/3 cup powdered sugar, sifted
1-3/4 cups all-purpose flour
Pinch of salt
3 tablespoons dry custard mix
15 candied cherries, cut in half

To Finish:
Sifted powdered sugar for sprinkling

Preheat oven to 350F (175C). Grease several baking sheets with butter; dust lightly with flour. In a medium-size bowl, beat butter with powdered sugar until very light and creamy. Sift flour, salt and custard mix into bowl; mix into butter with a wooden spoon to form a soft dough.

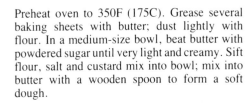

Put dough in a piping bag fitted with a 1/2-inch (10-point-star) tip. Pipe shell shapes onto prepared baking sheets, spacing well apart. Place half a candied cherry on pointed end of each shell.

Bake about 20 minutes or until very lightly browned. Cool on baking sheets a few minutes then remove to wire racks to cool completely. When cool, sprinkle powdered sugar lightly over cookies.

Makes about 30 cookies.

Chocolate Dreams

1/2 cup butter, softened
1/4 cup sugar
1 egg, beaten
1-3/4 cups all-purpose flour
1/4 cup unsweetened cocoa
1/2 teaspoon baking powder
Pinch of salt

Glaze:
1 tablespoon milk
2 teaspoons superfine sugar, plus a little extra
    for sprinkling

Chocolate Filling:
1/3 cup whipping cream
3 oz. semisweet chocolate, chopped

Preheat oven to 350F (175C). Grease several baking sheets with butter. In a medium-size bowl, beat butter with sugar until creamy; beat in egg. Sift flour, cocoa, baking powder and salt into bowl; blend in with a spoon, then mix with your hand to form a dough. Roll out dough on a floured surface to 1/8-inch thickness. Using fancy 2-inch cookie cutters, cut out shapes from dough as desired; place on prepared baking sheets. Knead and roll out trimmings; cut out more shapes.

To make glaze, stir milk and superfine sugar together in a small bowl until sugar dissolves. Brush over cookies. Bake 10 minutes. Sprinkle with extra sugar; cool on wire racks. To make filling, put whipping cream and chocolate in a small saucepan and stir over low heat until chocolate melts; do not boil. Pour into a small bowl. Cool until almost set then beat until fluffy. Sandwich cookies together with a generous amount of filling. Leave in a cool place until filling sets.

Makes about 30 cookies.

Honey & Lemon Creams

2 cups self-rising flour
2 teaspoons baking soda
2 teaspoons ground allspice
1/4 cup sugar
1/2 cup butter, softened
1/3 cup clear honey

Lemon Cream:
1/4 cup unsalted butter, softened
3/4 cup powdered sugar, sifted
Finely grated peel of 1 lemon
1 egg yolk
1 tablespoon lemon juice

Preheat oven to 400F (205C). Grease several baking sheets; line with parchment or waxed paper. Put flour, baking soda, allspice and sugar in a medium-size bowl. Cut in butter until mixture resembles fine bread crumbs. In a small saucepan, heat honey until warm, but not hot. Pour into flour mixture; mix to form a dough. Shape dough into balls about the size of unshelled hazelnuts. Place on prepared baking sheets, spacing well apart.

Bake 8 to 10 minutes or until golden brown. Cool on baking sheets until firm then remove to wire racks to cool completely. To make Lemon Cream, beat butter with powdered sugar and lemon peel in a small bowl until creamy. Beat in egg yolk and lemon juice. Sandwich cookies together with Lemon Cream. Leave in a cool place until filling sets.

Makes about 28 cookies.

Christmas Tree Cookies

2/3 cup butter, softened
1/3 cup sugar
3 egg yolks
2 teaspoons orange flower water
2 cups all-purpose flour
1 teaspoon baking powder

Decoration:
2 egg whites
3 cups powdered sugar, sifted
Edible gold and white glitter
Thin ribbon, various colors

Preheat oven to 350F (175C). Grease several baking sheets with butter.

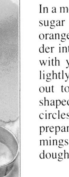

In a medium-size bowl, beat butter with 1/3 cup sugar until creamy. Beat in egg yolks and orange flower water. Sift flour and baking powder into bowl; blend in with a spoon then mix with your hand to form a soft dough. Knead lightly on a floured surface until smooth. Roll out to 1/8-inch thickness. Using 2-1/2-inch-shaped cookie cutters, cut out shapes such as circles, stars and hearts from dough. Place on prepared baking sheets. Knead and roll out trimmings; cut out more shapes. Continue until dough is used up.

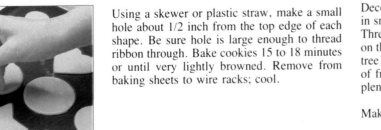

Using a skewer or plastic straw, make a small hole about 1/2 inch from the top edge of each shape. Be sure hole is large enough to thread ribbon through. Bake cookies 15 to 18 minutes or until very lightly browned. Remove from baking sheets to wire racks; cool.

To decorate cookies, mix egg whites with 2 cups of the powdered sugar in a medium-size bowl. Icing should be thick enough to coat the back of a spoon. Brush icing thinly and evenly over each cookie. Let icing set. Meanwhile, beat remaining powdered sugar into remaining icing, beating until icing forms stiff peaks. Cover with plastic wrap to prevent drying.

On two small saucers, blend gold and white glitter with water to make a smooth thin paste. Paint cookies with glitters. Allow to dry.

Decorate shapes with reserved icing by adding it in small flecks or by piping it on; let icing set. Thread cookies onto colored ribbons and hang on the Christmas tree. If cookies are left on the tree too long they will dry out. So keep a supply of fresh cookies in an airtight container to replenish the tree.

Makes about 28 Christmas Tree Cookies.

Advent Crescents

2 cups all-purpose flour
Pinch of salt
1/2 cup sugar
1-1/3 cups (5 oz.) ground almonds
1 cup butter, cut in small cubes
3 egg yolks
A few drops almond extract

To Finish:
Sifted powdered sugar for sprinkling

Sift flour and salt into a large bowl; mix in sugar and ground almonds. Make a well in the center.

Add butter, egg yolks and almond extract to the well. Using your fingertips, gently mix butter with egg yolks, gradually incorporating flour mixture until a soft dough forms. Wrap dough in plastic wrap; refrigerate 30 minutes. Preheat oven to 350F (175C).

Shape dough into walnut-size balls, then into thin rolls each about 4 inches long. Curve rolls into a crescent shape. Place on ungreased baking sheets. Bake crescents 15 minutes or until lightly browned. Cool on baking sheets. Sprinkle heavily with powdered sugar. Remove from baking sheets to a serving plate.

Makes about 42 crescents.

Brandy Shapes

1/2 cup butter, softened
3/4 cup sugar
2 teaspoons brandy
1 egg, beaten
2 cups all-purpose flour
Pinch of salt

To Decorate:
14 raisins
Sifted powdered sugar for sprinkling
1/3 cup powdered sugar, sifted
1 tablespoon lemon juice
Lemon-flavored fruit slices

Preheat oven to 375F (190C). Grease several baking sheets with butter. In a medium-size bowl, beat butter with sugar until very creamy.

Beat in brandy. Gradually beat in egg. Sift flour and salt into bowl; mix in with a wooden spoon to form a fairly stiff dough. Put mixture in a piping bag fitted with a 1/2-inch (10-point-star) tip. Pipe half of mixture onto prepared baking sheets in 2-inch-long "S" shapes, spacing well apart. Decorate with raisins. Pipe remaining mixture into rings.

Bake cookies about 15 minutes or until lightly browned. Remove from baking sheets to wire racks; cool. To decorate, sprinkle powdered sugar very lightly over "S" shapes. In a small bowl, blend 1/3 cup powdered sugar with lemon juice to make a thin icing. Brush over rings; decorate with fruit slices before icing sets.

Makes about 28 cookies.

Petit Lemon Cups

2 tablespoons unsalted butter
5 teaspoons sugar
1 tablespoon light corn syrup
Finely grated peel of 1/2 a lemon
1/4 cup all-purpose flour, sifted

Filling:
3 tablespoons unsalted butter
Finely grated peel of 1 lemon
1 tablespoon lemon juice
1 tablespoon dairy sour cream
1-1/2 cups powdered sugar, sifted

Put butter, sugar, corn syrup and lemon peel in a small saucepan and stir over medium heat until melted. Stir in flour. Set aside to cool.

Preheat oven to 375F (190C). Grease a large baking sheet; line with parchment or waxed paper. Using a round 1/4 teaspoon measuring spoon, spoon 12 tiny circles of mixture onto prepared baking sheet, spacing well apart. Bake 5 minutes or until lightly browned. Cool a few seconds. Lift rounds from baking sheet and place in miniature tart pans to mold into a cup shape. When cool, remove to a wire rack. Repeat until mixture is all used.

To make filling, place butter, lemon peel and juice in a small bowl set over a pan of gently simmering water; stir until butter melts. Remove from heat. Stir in sour cream and powdered sugar. Beat until cool and thickened. Spoon or pipe filling into center of each cup.

Makes about 40 cups.

Italian Cookies

2 eggs
2/3 cup sugar
Finely grated peel of 1 lemon
1 cup all-purpose flour, sifted
1/2 cup (2 oz.) pine nuts
1/3 to 1/2 cup powdered sugar

Grease several baking sheets; line with parchment or waxed paper. Put eggs, sugar and lemon peel in a small bowl. Place over a pan of gently simmering water; beat until very thick. Remove from heat. Continue beating until cool and the mixture retains its shape for a few seconds after spoon is drawn through it. Fold in flour.

Drop teaspoonfuls of mixture onto prepared baking sheets, spacing well apart; sprinkle with pine nuts. Let stand 15 minutes. Meanwhile, preheat oven to 350F (175C).

Sprinkle powdered sugar evenly over cookies. Bake about 15 minutes or until lightly browned. Let cool on baking sheets a few minutes, then remove to wire racks to cool completely. Store in an airtight container in a cool place for 3 to 4 days.

Makes about 44 cookies.

Decorative Bread Rings

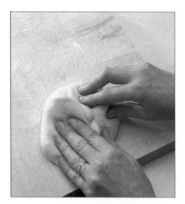

2 cups all-purpose flour, sifted
1/2 teaspoon superfine sugar
1/2 teaspoon salt
1 tablespoon butter
1 teaspoon active dry yeast
1/2 cup warm water
1 egg yolk
1 teaspoon water
Red and green food coloring, if desired
Colored ribbon

In a bowl, combine sifted flour, sugar and salt. Cut butter into flour mixture finely. Stir in yeast and enough warm water to form a soft dough. Knead on a lightly floured surface until smooth and no longer sticky or use a food processor fitted with a plastic blade.

Return dough to bowl. Cover with plastic wrap and let stand 5 minutes. Re-knead dough until smooth. Cut off 1/4 of dough and reserve. Shape remainder in a 24-inch roll. Cut roll in half. Shape in rings by joining ends together. Seal with water and place on a floured baking sheet. Cover and let stand in a warm place to rise 20 to 30 minutes. Meanwhile, roll out remaining dough very thinly. Using a holly cutter, cut out about 40 holly leaves and mark veins with a knife. Shape 40 beads of dough for berries. Arrange on a floured plate. Cover with plastic wrap and place in a cool place. Preheat oven to 425F (220C).

Divide egg yolk among 3 egg cups. Add water to 1 and brush dough rings to glaze. Add green food coloring to 1 and red to other cup. Bake dough rings 10 to 15 minutes or until risen but pale in color. Remove rings from oven. Arrange holly leaves and berries on rings. Glaze leaves green and berries red and return rings to oven 5 to 6 minutes until glaze has set. Cool on a wire rack. Tie with ribbon to use as decorations or serve as bread. Makes 2 rings.

Chocolate Decorations

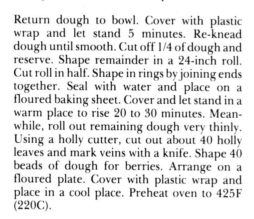

4 (1-oz.) squares semi-sweet chocolate
8 (1-oz.) squares white chocolate
Pink, green and yellow oil-based or powdered food colorings
Pink, green and yellow fine ribbon

Break up each chocolate and place in separate bowls set over saucepans of hand-hot water. Stir occasionally until melted. Divide 1/2 of white chocolate into 3 bowls. Color each pink, green and yellow with food colorings.

Draw around novelty cookie cutters on parchment paper. Half-fill 2 small pastry bags with dark chocolate. Snip a small point off 1 bag and pipe a fine outline of chocolate following shapes. Fill center of each shape with remaining dark chocolate, snipping a larger point off end so that shapes look over-filled and rounded.

Repeat to make different shaped chocolate decorations, using white and some colored chocolate as above. Let stand until hard. Carefully peel off paper, taking care not to mark surface. Sandwich matching shapes together with melted chocolate, placing ribbon loops in between. Decorate shapes with piped colored chocolate using a small pastry bag with end snipped off. Pipe lines, dots, zig-zags, lattice or write Christmas messages. Allow all decorations to dry before hanging up with ribbons. Makes about 20 decorations.

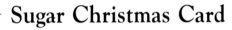

Sugar-Crystal Decorations

1-3/4 cups superfine sugar
3 to 4 teaspoons cold water
Blue, pink, green and yellow food colorings
Colored fine ribbons

Place sugar in a bowl. Add a little cold water at a time, stirring with a fork, until sugar is like damp sand. Divide sugar among 5 bowls. Leave 1 white and tint remaining 4 pale blue, pink, green and yellow.

Using plastic Christmas decoration mold shapes or figures, fill 1 shape at a time and press firmly to pack well. To insert ribbon for hanging decorations, place a loop of ribbon when mold is only half-filled, then fill to top and press down well. Or make a hole with a skewer when sugar has almost set. Repeat filling molds with colored sugar. Place a flat tray over top of molds and invert. Lift off molds and leave sugar shapes to dry in a warm place.

Fill larger molds like bells, cones or half egg shells with sugar and pack well. Invert on a tray. Let stand until sugar has set forming a crust. Return shape to mold. Scoop out sugar from center leaving a hollow shape. Make holes for ribbons with skewer. Remove from molds and let dry. Thread ribbons through to hang sugar decorations. Try decorating or painting using a fine paint brush and food colorings or food coloring pens. Makes about 25 decorations.

Sugar Christmas Card

1 teaspoon plain gelatin
1 tablespoon cold water
1 teaspoon liquid glucose
1 teaspoon shortening
1-1/2 cups powdered sugar, sifted
1/2 teaspoon gum tragacanth
1/2 egg white
Green and red food colorings
Powdered sugar icing
Assorted colors food coloring pens
Assorted colors fine ribbon

Sprinkle gelatin over cold water and soften 2 to 3 minutes. Stand bowl in a saucepan of hot water and stir until dissolved and hot. Add liquid glucose and shortening; stir until melted. Combine powdered sugar, gum tragacanth, egg white and gelatin mixture to form a soft paste.

Knead on a surface lightly dusted with powdered sugar until sugar paste is white and smooth. Keep sealed in a plastic bag until needed. Thinly roll out about 1/3 of sugar paste and cut out 2 (3-inch) squares. Flute or scallop edges on 3 sides of both pieces using a small cutter or icing crimper. Using a tiny round cutter or end of a pastry nozzle, cut out small rounds in between scalloped edges. Cut 2 large holes down side of plain edge evenly spaced apart from center with small cutter on both pieces. Dry on a flat surface sprinkled with cornstarch .

Color trimmings with red and green food colorings. Make tiny berries from red icing. Roll and cut out holly leaves from green icing. Mark veins with a knife and let dry. Thread ribbon in and out of the holes around edges. Attach holly leaves and berries on front of card with powdered sugar icing. Draw a design with food coloring pens and write a message on inside of card. Tie 2 pieces of card together with ribbon to join card. Makes about 6 cards.

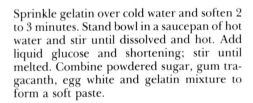

Fondant Sweets

8 oz. ready-to-roll fondant icing (sugar paste)
Pink, green, yellow, violet and orange food
  colorings

Flavorings:
3 pieces marrons glacés
3 pieces crystallized ginger
1/2 teaspoon peppermint oil
1 teaspoon finely grated orange peel
1 teaspoon finely grated lemon peel
1 teaspoon finely grated lime peel

Cut fondant in 6 pieces. Tint 5 pieces very pale pink, green, yellow, violet and orange.

Cut 2 marrons glacés and pink fondant in 8 pieces. Wrap each piece of marron glacé in pink fondant and shape in a smooth ball. Repeat with violet fondant and crystallized ginger to make oval shaped sweets. Decorate tops with remaining marron glacé and crystallized ginger.

Flavor white fondant with a few drops of peppermint oil. Roll out to 1/4-inch thickness. Using a small round or crescent cutter, cut out about 8 to 10 shapes. Knead orange peel into orange fondant, lemon peel into yellow fondant and lime peel into green fondant. Shape each piece in tiny pinwheels, squares or diamond shapes. Place all fondants on a parchment paper-lined baking sheet to dry out completely. Makes 40 pieces.

Hand-Dipped Chocolates

3 oz. ready-to-roll fondant icing (sugar paste)
Rose and violet flavorings
Pink and violet food colorings
2 oz. white marzipan
6 Brazil nuts
6 whole almonds
6 (1-oz.) squares semi-sweet chocolate
6 (1-oz.) squares white chocolate
6 (1-oz.) squares milk chocolate
6 maraschino cherries
6 creme de menthe cherries
Crystallized rose and violet petals

Cut fondant in 2 pieces. Flavor 1 piece rose and color pale pink with food coloring. Flavor remaining piece violet and color pale mauve with food coloring.

Roll out fondant to 1/2-inch thickness. Cut in shapes using cocktail cutters. Place on a waxed paper-lined baking sheet. Shape marzipan in various shapes by rolling bite-sized pieces between hands in balls, logs or ovals. Arrange on a baking sheet. Let dry several hours or overnight. Toast nuts until golden brown.

Melt each chocolate in different bowls over hand-hot water, stirring until melted. Using a fork, dip 1 center at a time into chocolate. Tap to remove excess and place chocolate on parchment paper-lined baking sheets. Leave plain, mark top with a fork or decorate rose and violet centers with crystallized petals. Continue to dip all centers, using white, dark or milk chocolate. Using a pastry bag, pipe some chocolates with threads of chocolate. Makes 30 pieces.

Marzipan

2 cups ground almonds
1¾ cup powdered sugar, sifted
2 teaspoons lemon juice
2 teaspoons sherry or brandy
2 drops almond extract, if desired
2 small egg whites
powdered sugar

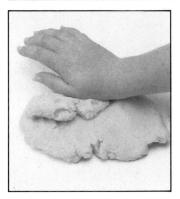

Combine almonds and sugar in a medium bowl. Add lemon juice, sherry or brandy, and almond extract, if desired.

Gradually mix in enough egg white to ensure that paste is sticky, but not wet.

Knead paste until smooth on a pastry board dusted with powdered sugar. Wrap in plastic wrap. Store in refrigerator up to 4 weeks. To use, see pages 78 and 86.

Makes 1 pound.

Marzipan Cherry Delights

3½ oz marzipan, see left
pink food coloring
1 teaspoon kirsch
3oz semisweet chocolate, chopped
6 peeled pistachio nuts

Line a plate with waxed paper. Knead marzipan with food coloring to shade of pale pink. Add sufficient kirsch so marzipan is slightly sticky but able to hold a shape. Form into 18 small balls. Place on waxed paper and refrigerate until firm.

Melt chocolate in a bowl or top of a double boiler set over a pan of simmering water. Stir until smooth. Insert a toothpick in top of each marzipan ball. Dip ½ of ball into chocolate. Place balls on waxed paper and refrigerate to dry and firm.

Cut pistachio nuts in 3 pieces lengthwise. Remove toothpicks and insert pistachio nuts in cavity left by toothpick. Store in a covered container in refrigerator up to 10 days.

Makes 18 balls.

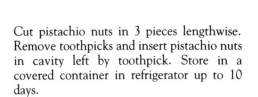

Marzipan Fruits

1¼ cups finely ground almonds
¾ cup powdered sugar (or more, if a sweeter flavor is desired)
1 egg white
Red, green, blue and yellow food coloring
A few cloves

In a heatproof bowl or top of a double boiler placed over a saucepan of hot-water, place almonds; heat gently stirring occasionally until warmed. Remove double boiler from heat, add sugar and egg white.

On a work surface, knead almond mixture until a smooth, fairly dry paste. Roll into a ball, cover with a cloth and let stand at room temperature for 15 minutes.

Break off small portions and shape into desired 'fruit'. The exact size of the fruit is up to you, but they should never be larger than a small walnut. You will need a couple of fine-pointed brushes, a saucer for mixing colors, a cup of water and a cloth for wiping brushes between color changes. Remember, red and yellow make orange, diluted orange will put the base color on peaches, red and green make brown for the stripes on bananas. Use cloves for the stem ends of oranges, pears and apples. You may make leaves from marzipan or use angelica.

Makes about ½ lb.

Caramelized Fruits

⅔ cup sugar
5 tablespoons water
Warm water
About 2 cups fresh assorted fruit, such as grapes. tangerine sections and strawberries, rinsed if necessary

In a heavy-bottomed saucepan combine sugar and water. Cook over a gentle heat, stirring occasionally until sugar is dissolved.

Bring to boil without stirring; boil until mixture turns a pale caramel color. Remove immediately from heat; place in a bowl of warm water.

Carefully place individual pieces of fruit in caramel; coating completely. Set fruit onto lightly greased cookie sheet or wire rack. Allow to cool and harden. To serve, place in petit four cases. Fruit must be eaten within 24 hours. Do not refrigerate.

Makes about 1½ lbs.

Spiced Dried Fruit

1 cup sugar
1½ teaspoons grated lemon peel
1 teaspoon powdered cinnamon
¼ teaspoon powdered cloves
¼ teaspoon powdered nutmeg
¾ cup water
5 oz dried apricots, pears or apples
Powdered sugar

In a saucepan, combine sugar, lemon peel, spices and water. Cook over a low heat, stirring constantly, until sugar dissolves. Increase the heat, bring to a boil without stirring. Boil to soft ball stage, 240F (117C) on candy thermometer.

Add fruit and cook slowly 5 minutes, stirring to avoid burning. Remove saucepan and immediately place it in a pan of warm water.

Using a fork, carefully lift out individual pieces of fruit, draining them over the pan. Roll fruit pieces immediately in powdered sugar. Package in jars or decorative boxes.

Makes about ½ lb.

Apricot Balls

½ cup dried apricots, chopped
½ cup pitted prunes, chopped
¼ cup raisins, chopped
3 tablespoons Cointreau or other orange liqueur
2 teaspoons grated orange peel
1⅓ cup shredded coconut
¾ cup chopped walnuts
¾ cup sugar

In a bowl, combine apricots, prunes and raisins, sprinkle with Cointreau. Allow fruit to macerate at room temperature 1 hour, stirring occasionally.

In a food processor or blender, finely chop the fruit. In a bowl, combine chopped fruit, grated orange peel, ⅔ cup coconut and walnuts; mix thoroughly.

On a plate combine sugar and remaining coconut. Form fruit mixture into small, bite-size balls and roll in sugar and coconut mixture. Store in an airtight container with wax paper between layers.

Makes 24 to 30 balls.

Lemon Drops

½ cup water
1 ⅓ cups sugar
¼ teaspoon cream of tartar
½ teaspoon lemon extract
Powdered sugar

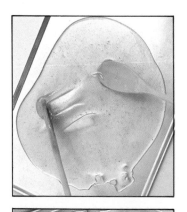

In a large heavy-bottomed saucepan, combine water and sugar, cook over medium heat stirring to dissolve sugar. Bring to boil. Add cream of tartar and continue boiling until syrup reaches soft crack stage, 270F (140C) on candy thermometer. Remove immediately from heat – syrup should stay a pale yellow color. Add lemon extract and tartaric acid. Pour syrup onto an oiled slab or into a dish.

Using two wooden spoons, work into a toffee. Continue working until toffee becomes cool enough to handle with oiled hands. Pull toffee into a long roll.

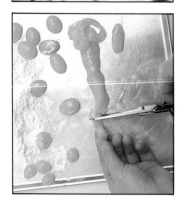

With oiled scissors, cut off small pieces and shape with your hands into drops. Coat with powdered sugar and allow the drops to cool and dry thoroughly. Store in airtight containers.

Makes about ½ lb.

Praline

⅓ cup almond slivers or hazelnuts
½ cup sugar
¼ cup water

Place nuts on a baking sheet and toast at 350F (180C) for 10 minutes or until golden brown. Stir occasionally to color evenly. If using hazelnuts, chop finely. Lightly oil another baking sheet. In a medium saucepan, heat sugar and water over low heat until sugar dissolves, shaking pan occasionally. Increase heat and cook until golden and sugary. Stir in nuts.

Cook 2–3 minutes, stirring well.

Pour onto prepared sheet; cool. When brittle, finely crush with a meat mallet or process in a blender or processor. Store in an airtight container in refrigerator 3 weeks.

Makes ¾ cup crushed praline.

Nut Toffees

2 cups sugar
1/2 cup butter, chopped
2 tablespoons white vinegar
2 tablespoons boiling water
Assortment of unsalted nuts, such as pecans, almonds, walnuts and pistachio nuts

In a heavy-bottomed saucepan, combine sugar, butter, vinegar and boiling water. Place over a low heat and stir until sugar is dissolved. Increase the heat; cook without stirring until mixture changes color. Start testing by spooning mixture by drops into a small bowl of iced water. When a firm ball is produced (test by feeling), toffee is done. Or cook to 290F (147C) on candy thermometer.

Pour into a well-buttered 9-inch square pan. Let cool.

Mark into pieces with a sharp knife. Place nuts in each square. Let cool completely and harden. Turn out onto a wooden board and break into pieces. Wrap in foil or plastic wrap.

Makes about 1 lb.

Mixed Toffees

4 1/2 cups sugar
1 cup butter
1/4 cup white vinegar
4 tablespoons boiling water
Glacé cherries and nuts, for decoration

In a large heavy-bottomed saucepan, bring sugar, butter, vinegar and water to a boil.

Boil until the color changes and then start testing by dropping the mixture by drops into a teacup or glass of iced water. When a firm ball is produced (test by feeling) toffee is done. Or cook to 290F (147C) on candy thermometer. Spoon immediately into small candy molds.

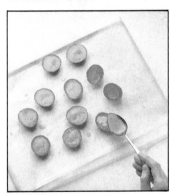

Decorate with cherries and nuts.

Makes about 24.

Almond Praline Truffles

1/3 cup butter, cubed
1/2 cup (4 fl oz) whipping cream
10 oz milk chocolate, chopped
2 egg yolks
3/4 cup crushed almond praline, see page 80
unsweetened cocoa powder

In a small saucepan, combine butter with cream. Cook on low heat until butter melts and cream bubbles around edges.

Remove from heat; add chocolate. Cover and let stand until chocolate melts. Stir until smooth. Add egg yolks, one at a time. Stir over a low heat until glossy. Mixture should be tepid. Remove from heat; cool. Fold in crushed praline. Refrigerate until firm.

Form into 60 balls. Roll in cocoa and coat completely. Chill until firm. Refrigerate in an airtight container up to 10 days. To serve, place in small paper or foil cases.

Makes 60 truffles.

Hazelnut Praline Truffles

1/4 cup butter, cubed
8oz semisweet chocolate, chopped
1/2 cup (4 fl oz) whipping cream
1 tablespoon dark rum
3/4 cup hazelnut praline, see page 80

TO COAT: 1 1/2 oz semisweet chocolate, chopped
1 1/2 oz milk chocolate, chopped

Melt butter in a small saucepan. Remove from heat and add chocolate. Cover and let stand 3 minutes. Stir until smooth. Add cream a few spoonfuls at a time, stirring well until chocolate is smooth.

Cool mixture. Add rum. Mix in crushed hazelnut praline and stir well. Refrigerate until firm. Form into 60 small balls. Refrigerate to firm.

To coat the truffles, melt semisweet chocolate in a bowl or top of a double boiler set over a pan of simmering water. Stir until smooth. Repeat procedure for milk chocolate. Dip tops of 30 truffles into semisweet chocolate. Dip the tops of remaining 30 into milk chocolate. Place on waxed paper, chocolate side uppermost. Let set at room temperature. Refrigerate in a covered container with waxed paper between layers up to 10 days.

Makes about 60 truffles.

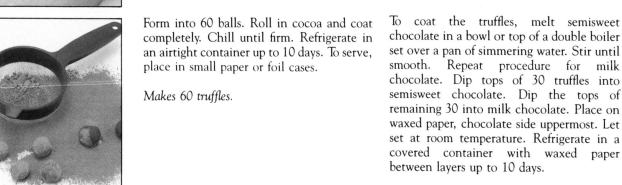

Plain Génoise

3 eggs
½ cup superfine sugar
1 teaspoon vanilla extract
¾ cup all-purpose flour, sifted
2 tablespoons butter, melted and cooled

Preheat oven to 350F (180C). Grease and flour bottom and sides of a 14″ x 10″ baking pan. Shake out excess flour.

Combine eggs and sugar in a medium mixing bowl. Place bowl in a pan of hot water. Beat until mixture is very thick and just warm. Mixture should form a ribbon when beaters are lifted. Remove from heat and add vanilla. Continue beating until mixture is almost cool. Fold flour into egg and sugar mixture. Mix in butter.

Pour batter into prepared greased pan; level top. Bake in a preheated oven 20-25 minutes or until set on top. Cool pan on a wire rack 10 minutes. Run a knife carefully around the edge. Remove from pan. Cool completely on wire rack. Use within 36 hours or wrap and freeze up to 6 weeks.

Makes one 14″ x 10″ cake.

Orange Truffles

¼ cup butter, chopped
⅓ cup (2½ fl oz) whipping cream
7 oz semisweet chocolate, chopped
1 egg yolk
1 teaspoon grated orange peel
2 tablespoons finely chopped mixed citrus peel
2 tablespoons Grand Marnier
unsweetened cocoa powder

In a small saucepan, combine butter and cream. Cook on low heat until butter melts and cream bubbles around edge. Remove from heat; add chocolate. Cover and let stand until chocolate melts. Stir until smooth.

Stir in egg yolk. Mix in orange peel, citrus peel, and Grand Marnier. Chill until firm.

Form into 40 balls. Roll in cocoa. Refrigerate in an airtight container up to 2 weeks. To serve, place in small paper or foil cases.

Makes 40 truffles.

Rum Balls

RUM BALLS: ³/4 cup génoise crumbs, see page 83
¹/4 cup powdered sugar
¹/4 cup ground almonds
2 teaspoons dark rum
1 teaspoon lemon juice
1¹/2 oz semisweet chocolate, chopped
2 tablespoons whipping cream

ICING: ¹/3 cup powdered sugar
2 tablespoons butter, chopped
1 oz semisweet chocolate, grated
2 teaspoons dark rum
warm water

TO DECORATE: chocolate sprinkles

In a medium bowl, combine cake crumbs, sugar, almonds, rum and lemon juice. Melt chocolate in a bowl or top of a double boiler set over a pan of simmering water. Add to rum mixture with sufficient cream for mixture to hold together when pressed between fingers. Form teaspoonfuls of mixture into 18 small balls. Refrigerate on a baking sheet 4 hours or until firm.

To make icing, combine sugar, butter, chocolate and rum in a small saucepan. When chocolate and butter softens, add a tablespoon of water. Warm again and add sufficient water to liquify.

To coat rum balls, insert a poultry skewer in center of a rum ball. Tilt pan of icing and dip each ball. Let excess drip. To decorate, roll in chocolate sprinkles to coat completely. Refrigerate in a covered container with waxed paper between layers up to 10 days.

Makes 18 rum balls.

Christmas Truffles

³/4 cup (3 oz) vanilla cookies, crushed
2 tablespoons finely chopped glacé cherries
2 tablespoons finely chopped hazelnuts
2 tablespoons ground almonds
2 tablespoons finely chopped mixed citrus peel
2 tablespoons chopped raisins
1 tablespoon brandy or rum
2 drops almond extract
¹/4 cup (2 oz) butter, cubed
6 oz semisweet chocolate, chopped
2 tablespoons whipping cream

TO COAT: ³/4 cup (3 oz) finely chopped hazelnuts

In a medium bowl, mix cookies, cherries, hazelnuts, almonds, peel, raisins, brandy or rum and almond extract.

Melt butter in a small saucepan until bubbling. Add chocolate; remove from heat. Cover and let stand. Stir occasionally, until chocolate melts. Add cream; stir into cookie mixture. Refrigerate until firm.

Form into 40 small balls. To coat, roll balls in nuts. Refrigerate in a covered container with waxed paper between layers up to 2 weeks. To serve, place in small paper or foil cases.

Makes 40 truffles.

Grand Marnier Petits Fours

¹/₃ plain génoise, see page 83
GRAND MARNIER CREAM: ¼ cup unsalted butter
3 tablespoons powdered sugar
½ teaspoon grated orange peel
1 egg yolk
1 tablespoon Grand Marnier
ICING: 1 tablespoon light corn syrup
3 tablespoons water
1 tablespoon Grand Marnier
2 cups powdered sugar
yellow food coloring
TO DECORATE: angelica strips

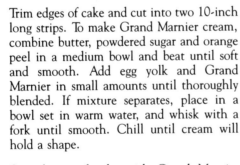

Trim edges of cake and cut into two 10-inch long strips. To make Grand Marnier cream, combine butter, powdered sugar and orange peel in a medium bowl and beat until soft and smooth. Add egg yolk and Grand Marnier in small amounts until thoroughly blended. If mixture separates, place in a bowl set in warm water, and whisk with a fork until smooth. Chill until cream will hold a shape.

Spread top of cake with Grand Marnier cream. Place remaining cream in a piping bag with a star tube and decorate cake. Chill cake until cream is hard. Cut each strip of cake into 10 pieces. Place cakes on a wire rack set over a jelly-roll pan.

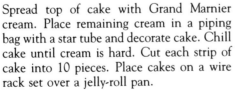

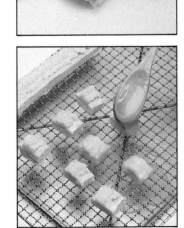

To make icing, cook corn syrup and water in a medium saucepan until corn syrup has melted and water is just bubbling. Stir in Grand Marnier and powdered sugar. Remove from heat and beat until smooth. Reheat until tepid. If icing is too thick, add 1 teaspoon of water. Tint icing with yellow food coloring. Spoon icing over cakes. Let stand until icing is set. Decorate with angelica strips.

Makes 20 petits fours.

Nut Cakes with Lemon Syrup

¼ cup (1 oz) ground walnuts
¼ cup (1 oz) ground almonds
1 tablespoon finely-crushed vanilla cookies
grated peel of ½ lemon
1 egg yolk
2 tablespoons superfine sugar
1 egg white
LEMON SYRUP: ¼ cup sugar
1 tablespoon lemon juice
¼ cup (2 fl oz) water
1 tablespoon dark or white rum
TOPPING: ¼ cup (3 oz) apricot jam
2 teaspoons lemon juice
TO DECORATE: walnut pieces or almond flakes

Preheat oven to 350F (180C). Grease 12 miniature tart pans. In a small bowl, mix nuts with cookie crumbs. Add lemon peel. In a small bowl, beat egg yolk with sugar until fluffy. In a small bowl beat egg white until stiff. Fold into egg yolk mixture. Add dry ingredients to eggs, ½ at a time. Fold in gently. Fill tart pans ¾ full of batter. Bake in preheated oven 15 minutes or until firm. Cool 2 minutes before soaking with syrup.

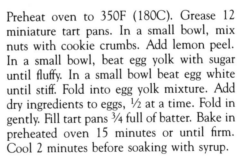

To make syrup, in a small saucepan, bring sugar, lemon juice and water to the boil over medium heat. Simmer 1 minute. Remove from heat. Add rum; cool until tepid. Pour syrup over cakes while still in tart pans. Cool cakes completely. Carefully run a knife around edge to remove cake from tart pan. Place on a wire rack set over a baking sheet.

To make topping, in a small saucepan, heat the jam and lemon juice. Sieve if lumpy. Warm before brushing over top of cakes. Decorate with a walnut piece or almond flake. Let stand 6 hours. Store covered up to 48 hours.

Makes 12 cakes.

Christmas Puddings

¾ cup finely chopped dried figs
½ cup ground almonds
2 tablespoons powdered sugar
2 oz semisweet chocolate, grated
2 teaspoons brandy
2 teaspoons lemon juice
1 egg white
TOPPING: 1 tablespoon whipping cream
2 oz white chocolate
1 teaspoon brandy
TO DECORATE: marzipan, page 77, green food coloring, 1 red glacé cherry

In a medium mixing bowl, mix figs, almonds, sugar, semisweet chocolate, brandy and lemon juice. Add egg white, a teaspoon at a time, to bind mixture. Chill 2 hours. Form a small walnut sized ball. Roll in palm of hand until smooth. Using a very sharp knife, cut off ⅓ of ball so ball will sit flat. Repeat, returning extra piece to mixture each time. Refrigerate in a covered container up to 2 weeks.

To make topping, heat cream in a small saucepan until bubbling. Remove from heat and add chocolate. Cover and let stand 5 minutes. Add brandy. Stir until smooth. Trickle topping over each pudding to simulate custard.

To decorate, add green food coloring to marzipan; knead well. Pinch off 40 tiny pieces. Roll each piece into a rectangle. To make leaves, press center of each rectangle and flatten, leaving end as a point. Curve each leaf slightly. Let dry 2 hours. Cut glacé cherry into small pieces. Place 2 leaves on top of each pudding and piece of cherry in center. Refrigerate in a single layer until puddings are firm, or up to 1 week.

Makes 20 puddings.

Nut Snowballs

¼ cup finely ground almonds
¼ cup finely ground hazelnuts
¾ cup powdered sugar
1 egg white

TO COAT: 2 egg whites
powdered sugar

Preheat oven to 350F (180C). Line bottom of baking sheet with waxed paper. In a small bowl, mix nuts together. Add sugar; gradually add sufficient egg white to form a paste.

Wet hands; form nut paste into 24 small round balls. In a small bowl whisk 2 egg whites lightly until slightly frothy. Dip balls into egg whites; roll in powdered sugar to coat.

Place in paper cases on baking sheet and bake 12 to 15 minutes or until golden on top and firm to touch. Remove from baking sheet; cool on a wire rack 12 hours. Dust with a little extra powdered sugar. Store in an airtight container up to 1 week.

Makes 24 snowballs.

Mushroom Meringues

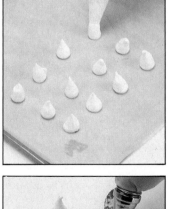

2 egg whites
pinch of salt
¼ teaspoon cream of tartar
⅓ cup superfine sugar
1 teaspoon vanilla extract
unsweetened cocoa powder, sifted

FILLING: ½ cup (4 fl oz) whipping cream
1 oz milk chocolate, chopped
2 teaspoons brandy

Preheat oven to 300F (150C). Line 2 baking sheets with parchment paper. In a small mixing bowl, beat egg whites with salt and cream of tartar until stiff. Gradually add sugar and vanilla extract and beat to a very stiff meringue. To form caps, spoon ⅔ meringue into a pastry bag fitted with a plain nozzle. Pipe 40 small mounds onto paper-lined baking sheet. Dust tops with cocoa.

Spoon remaining meringue into a pastry bag fitted with a plain nozzle. Pipe 40 mushroom stalks on second paper-lined baking sheet. Bake meringues in preheated oven 10 minutes. Adjust oven temperature to 250F (120C). Bake stalks 1–1½ hours, caps 1½–2 hours until very crisp. Cool on baking sheets on wire racks. Remove cooled meringues from paper. Store in an airtight container.

To make filling, warm cream in a small saucepan. Add chocolate to cream; stir until melted. Add brandy; cool mixture before refrigerating. When mixture is completely cold, whisk gently until soft peaks form. Place filling in bottom of each meringue cap and insert a stalk. Serve immediately.

Makes 40 mushrooms.

Tiny Meringues

2 egg whites
pinch of salt
¼ teaspoon cream of tartar
⅓ cup superfine sugar
1 teaspoon vanilla extract

FILLING: ½ cup whipped cream
blueberries, raspberries, redcurrants or baby strawberries

TO DECORATE: 30 small pieces of angelica or baby mint leaves

Preheat oven to 300F (150C). Line a baking sheet with parchment paper. Beat egg whites until stiff with salt and cream of tartar. Add ½ sugar and beat again. Add remainder of sugar and beat until very stiff. Add vanilla.

Form teaspoonfuls of meringue into 30 small flat buttons on paper-lined baking sheet. Spoon remaining meringue into small pastry bag fitted with a small fluted nozzle. Pipe around edge of circles, keeping well inside bottom to form a casing.

Bake meringues in preheated oven 10 minutes. Adjust oven temperature to 250F (120C). Bake until the meringues are crisp to touch and lightly colored. If meringues begin to darken, turn oven off and let stand to crisp. Cool on baking sheet on wire rack. Carefully remove cooled meringues from paper, Store in an airtight container up to 2 weeks. To fill meringues, spoon cream into a small pastry bag fitted with a fluted nozzle. Pipe a small rosette 'into the center of meringue. Top with blueberries, raspberries, red currants or a tiny strawberry. Decorate with angelica or mint leaves. Serve immediately.

Makes 30 meringues.

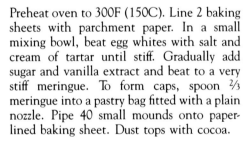
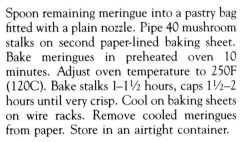

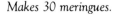

Satsuma & Pine Nut Conserve

9 satsumas (2 lb. total)
About 2-1/2 cups water
4 cups sugar
1/4 cup orange flower water
1/2 cup pine nuts

Scrub satsumas well. Using a potato peeler or sharp knife, pare peel from satsumas, not including white pith. Cut peel in fine strips. Place in a large saucepan with 2/3 cup of water. Bring to a boil, cover and cook gently 1 hour or until tender.

Cut satsumas in half. Squeeze juice into a 2-cup glass measure. Add enough water to make 1-3/4 cups, if necessary. Reserve all seeds and place in a piece of muslin; tie securely with a string. Place in a saucepan with satsuma peel. Bring to a boil. Cover and simmer 1 hour. Strain liquid from satsuma peel into saucepan with peel. Stir in sugar and juice. Bring to a boil, stirring constantly, until sugar has dissolved.

Boil rapidly 5 to 10 minutes until setting point is reached. To test, spoon some conserve onto a cold plate. Let stand a few minutes, then push with your finger. If surface wrinkles, setting point has been reached. Add orange flower water and pine nuts. Bring to a boil and boil 2 minutes. Cool 30 minutes. Meanwhile, sterilize 3 jars and lids. Stir conserve, then pour into warm jars. Cover each with paraffin and seal with lids. Store in a dry cool place. Makes 3 jars.

Brandied Mincemeat

6 cups raisins
3-1/3 cups currants
1 cup dried apricots
3/4 cup dates
1 cup candied peel
3/4 cup whole almonds
1 lb. cooking apples, peeled, cored
Finely grated peel and juice 2 lemons
2-1/4 cups light-brown sugar
1 cup unsalted butter, melted
1 tablespoon ground mixed spice
2/3 cup brandy

In a large bowl, place raisins and currants. Chop or mince apricots, dates, candied peel, almonds and apples. Add chopped fruit and nuts and lemon peel and juice to raisins and currants. Mix well. Stir in brown sugar, butter, mixed spice and brandy.

Stir mixture until evenly blended. Cover with plastic wrap and refrigerate 2 days.

Sterilize 6 (1-pint) jars and lids and keep warm. Stir mincemeat thoroughly, then spoon into hot jars, filling each to top. Cover each with paraffin and seal with lids. Makes 6 (1-pint) jars.

Spiced Citrus Slices

3 thin-skinned oranges
4 thin-skinned lemons
5 limes
Water
2-1/2 cups white wine vinegar
4-1/2 cups sugar
2 (2-inch) cinnamon sticks
2 teaspoons whole cloves
6 blades mace

Scrub fruit thoroughly. Cut each fruit in 1/8-inch thick slices. Lay slices in a stainless steel or enamel saucepan and just cover with water. Bring to a boil, cover and cook very gently about 10 minutes or until peel is tender. Drain slices and reserve liquor.

In another saucepan, gently heat vinegar, sugar and spices, stirring occasionally, until sugar has dissolved. Bring to a boil. Lay fruit slices in syrup. Add reserved liquor to cover fruit, if necessary, and cook very gently 15 minutes or until peel looks transparent.

Meanwhile, sterilize 3 small jars and lids. Arrange fruit slices in warm jars, alternating slices or packing each separately. Bring syrup to a boil. Immediately fill each jar to top and seal with lids. When cold, label and store in a cool place. Makes 3 small jars.

Lychees & Cherries in Chartreuse

10 fresh lychees or 1 (15-oz.) can lychees
2 cups fresh sweet cherries or 1 (15-oz.) can cherries
1 cup sugar
1-1/4 cups Chartreuse or Benedectine liqueur

Sterilize 3 or 4 small jars and lids and keep warm. Peel lychees and carefully remove pits, keeping fruit whole. Remove cherry stalks and pits. Wash cherries or drain canned fruit and dry on paper towels. Pierce skins of cherries all over with a clean needle or fine skewer.

Arrange 1 layer of cherries in 1 warm jar and sprinkle with a layer of sugar. Arrange 1 layer of lychees on top and sprinkle with more sugar. Continue to layer cherries, sugar and lychees until jar is loosely filled to neck of jar. Do not pack fruit tightly. Sprinkle with a final layer of sugar.

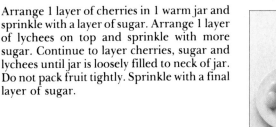

Fill jar to top with liqueur and seal with a clean lid. Repeat to fill more small jars with remaining fruit, sugar and liqueur. Store in a cool dry place up to 6 months. Makes 3 or 4 small jars.

Peach Chutney

2 lb. peaches, peeled, pitted and chopped
1 lb. onions, chopped
1 ¼ cups red wine vinegar
⅓ cup chopped, pitted dates
⅓ cup white raisins
1 teaspoon salt
½ teaspoon powdered ginger
½ teaspoon powdered cinnamon
¼ teaspoon powdered cloves
1 tablespoon mustard seeds
Grated peel and juice of 1 lemon
1 ½ cups packed brown sugar

In a large saucepan combine peaches with remaining ingredients, except sugar. Bring to a boil over high heat, stirring occasionally. Reduce heat and simmer peaches and onions until tender, stirring occasionally.

Add sugar and stir until dissolved. Simmer 2 to 3 hours, stirring frequently to prevent scorching, or until chutney is a rich brown color and thick.

Fill sterilized jars with chutney to within ¼-in of top. Seal with sterilized vinegar-proof lids. Process 15 minutes in boiling-water bath for 1-pint containers. (Place jars on a rack in processing pan. Do not allow jars to touch. Keep covered with 2-inches boiling water while processing.) Store in a cool, dark place – allow to mellow 6 weeks before using.

Makes about 3 pints.

Horseradish Mustard

¼ cup dry mustard
2 tablespoons grated fresh horseradish
1 teaspoon salt
¼ cup white vinegar
1 tablespoon olive oil

In a food processor or blender combine all ingredients.

Process until a smooth paste is formed.

When smooth, pour into a sterilized jar and seal. Store in the refrigerator – allow to mellow 2 weeks before using.

Makes about ¾ cup.

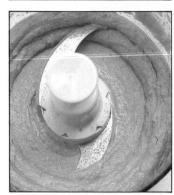

Mint Jelly

6 lb. tart green apples, quartered
Juice of 4 lemons
2 cups loosely packed fresh mint leaves
1 cup white wine vinegar
Sugar, see recipe
Chopped fresh mint leaves
Green food coloring
Mint extract, if desired

In a large heavy-bottomed saucepan, combine apples, lemon juice, mint; just cover with water. Simmer until apples are very soft. Add vinegar; simmer 5 minutes more.

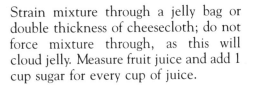

Strain mixture through a jelly bag or double thickness of cheesecloth; do not force mixture through, as this will cloud jelly. Measure fruit juice and add 1 cup sugar for every cup of juice.

In a clean pan, cook juice and sugar over a low heat until sugar dissolves, stirring. Increase heat, boil briskly 5 minutes, without stirring, until temperature reaches 220F (105C). Or, test using spoon method, page 93. Stir in chopped mint and a little coluring and 1 to 2 teaspoons mint extract if desired. Pour jelly to within 1/8-inch of top of sterilized jars. Cover, seal tightly with sterilized lids. Invert jars for a few seconds to complete seal. Store in a cool, dark place.

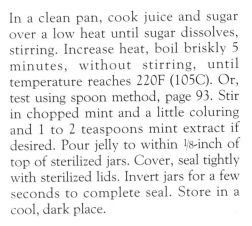

Makes 6 to 8 pints.

Sage and Apple Jelly

6 lb. tart apples, washed, quartered (do not peel or core)
Juice of 4 lemons
1 cup white wine vinegar
Sugar, see recipe
1 cup loosely packed chopped sage, washed
6-8 sprigs of sage

In a preserving pan or a large, heavy-bottomed saucepan, combine apples and lemon juice; add enough water to cover fruit. Simmer until the apples are soft. Add vinegar and bring to boil, boil 5 minutes.

Strain mixture through a jelly bag or double thickness of cheesecloth for an hour. Do not press any apples through bag as this will cause jelly to cloud. Measure fruit mixture and add 1 cup of sugar for every cup of juice. Pour back into preserving pan, bring to boil, stirring until sugar dissolves. Boil until temperature reaches 220F (105C). Or, test using spoon method, page 93. Stir in chopped sage.

Add sprigs of sage to sterilized jars. Pour jelly to within 1/8-inch of top of jars. Cover, seal tightly with sterilized lids. Invert jars for a few seconds to complete seal. Cool in upright position. Store in a cool, dark place.

Makes 6 to 8 pints.

Macedoine of Fruit in Brandy

1lb. mixed berries such as strawberries, raspberries, blueberries and gooseberries; rinsed
2lb. sugar
Approximately 2 cups brandy
1lb. mixed peeled, pitted peaches, plums, nectarines and apricots; halved

In a sterilized preserving jar, layer berries with sugar.

Pour brandy over to cover.

Layer peach, plum, nectarine and apricot halves with remaining sugar over berries. Pour brandy over to cover. Continue layering to ½-inch from top of jar. Seal. Process 30 minutes in boiling-water bath for 1-pint containers (place jars on rack in processing pan. Do not allow jars to touch. Keep covered with 2 inches boiling water while processing.) Store in a cool, dark place – allow to mellow at least 2 months before using.

Honey and Apricot Spread

12 dried apricots
1 cup creamed honey

In a bowl, place apricots, cover with boiling water; allow to stand at room temperature until softened.

Drain apricots. In blender or food processor, process apricots and honey.

When thoroughly combined, pour into a sterilized jar, seal with a sterilized lid; cool. Store in the refrigerator – allow to mellow 24 hours before using. You can easily double or triple this recipe.

Makes about 2 cups.

Grapefruit Marmalade

4 lb. grapefruit, well scrubbed
6 to 9 cups sugar

Cut grapefruit into quarters, remove seeds and pithy centers. Put the seeds and centers in a 6-inch square of cheesecloth, tie into a bag. Peel grapefruit. Cut peel into julienne strips. Slice peeled fruit crosswise into thin slices. Separate slices into individual sections. Place fruit and bag in a large bowl; just cover with water. Soak 12 hours. Remove bag. In large preserving pan or saucepan, simmer fruit and soaking water 1 hour. For every cup of fruit and water add ¾ cup sugar. Bring to a boil; boil about 20 minutes or to proper consistency.

Test marmalade for doneness immediately after boiling. Proper consistency is reached when candy thermometer reaches 220F (105C). Or, test by spoon test. Pour a small amount of marmalade onto a cold plate. Let stand until cold. If marmalade forms a skin and wrinkles when pushed with a finger or spoon, it is ready. Remove pan from heat while test preserve is cooling.

Cool 10 minutes; stir gently to mix skin through the marmalade. Pour into sterilized jars to within ½-inch of top. Seal with sterilized lids. Invert jars for a few seconds. Cool in upright position. Store in cool, dark place.

Makes about 5 pints.

Rum and Plum Jam

2 lb. plums
2 lemons
5¾ cups sugar
2 tablespoons dark rum

Pit and finely chop the plums; squeeze juice from lemons. In a large heavy-bottomed saucepan combine fruit, sugar and lemon juice.

Bring to a boil over a low heat, stirring until sugar is dissolved. Increase the heat and boil 10 minutes, stirring to avoid burning. Begin testing for proper consistency. Proper consistency is reached when candy thermometer reaches 220F (105C).

Or, test using spoon method described in Grapefuit Marmalade, page 93. Remove pan from heat and stir in rum. Allow jam to stand 10 minutes, stirring at intervals so fruit doesn't sink. Pour to within 1/8-inch of top of sterilized jars. Seal tightly with sterilized lids. Invert jars for a few seconds to complete seal. Cool in an upright position. Store in a cool, dark place.

Makes about 4 pints.

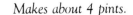

Old Fashioned Ginger Beer

2 lemons
3 cups sugar
1 oz piece fresh gingerroot, peeled and bruised
2 teaspoons cream of tartar
1½ tablespoons brewers yeast
5 quarts boiling water

Carefully remove peel from lemons; remove and discard all white pith. Slice lemons thinly, removing seeds.

In a large glass or earthenware bowl, place lemon slices, peel, sugar, ginger and cream of tartar. Pour boiling water over mixture; let stand until tepid. Add brewers yeast and let stand in a warm place for at least 24 hours, or up to 2 days.

Skim the yeast from the top and strain liquid through cheesecloth into sterilized bottles. Seal. Store in the refrigerator – allow to mellow 3 days before using.

Makes 5 quarts.

Coffee Liqueur

2 cups water
4½ cups sugar
4 teaspoons instant coffee powder
Few drops vanilla extract
1 cup brandy
1 cup rum

In a saucepan combine water, sugar, instant coffee and vanilla. Heat gently, stirring until sugar and coffee have dissolved. Cool.

Stir brandy and rum into syrup.

Into a large decanter, pour coffee liqueur. Seal. Store in a cool, dark place – allow to mellow 2 to 3 weeks before using.

Makes about 2 quarts.

Irish Cream Whiskey

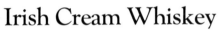

3 egg yolks
1 (14 oz.) can sweetened condensed milk
1¼ cups whipping cream
1½ cups whiskey
1½ tablespoons sweetened chocolate syrup
¼ teaspoon coconut extract

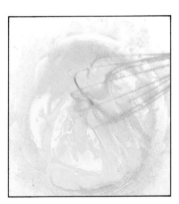

In a large bowl, beat egg yolks until thick.

Stir in condensed milk, cream, whiskey, chocolate syrup and coconut extract. Beat for 1 minute. Taste and add more coconut extract if desired.

In a large decanter pour Irish Cream Whiskey. Seal. Store in refrigerator – allow to mellow 7 days before using. Will keep up to 2 weeks.

Makes about 5 cups.

Peppermint Liqueur

1 cup water
2 cups sugar
1 teaspoon peppermint extract
1½ cups brandy
Approximately ½ teaspoon green food coloring

In a saucepan, combine water and sugar gently stirring. Heat until sugar dissolves. Cool.

Stir in peppermint extract, brandy and enough food coloring to make the syrup the color of crème de menthe. Pour into a sterilized decanter or bottle.

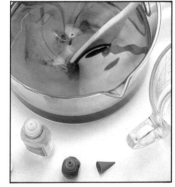

Seal and shake. Store in a cool dark place – allow to mellow 7 days before using.

Makes about 1 quart.

INDEX